For my parents, Bobbi and Wayne Mahood,
who taught us the joy of reading and writing,
and other acts of love and kindness.

Contents

Acknowledgments

A manuscript by a first timer requires an army of sympathetic soldiers. I asked a lot of mine. Not all can be noted but they all contributed in some significant way to the publication of this book. First, are the interviewees who gave their time generously and are my heroes. Behind the scenes, in no particular order, are my fallback and fall-forward editors, my father, Wayne Mahood, an accomplished author and his talented wife, Bobbi, my mom. My official copy editor, Cindy Black, who does amazing work. Todd and Patty Balf, our neighbors, authors and editors both, who made professional connections for me. My audio transcriber, friend, and fellow eco-warrior, Becca Marasco, who somehow made sense of each interview. Faithful reader, Barb McGrath, my brother-in-law's wife, gave me the approbation I desperately needed at various points. Gina Poirier of Gina Poirier Design. Long-term friends, Paul and Robin Satryb, were an endless stream of encouragement and editorial advice. My brother, Bruce Mahood, who offered support as only an older brother can. Nicole Crawford and Shelia Lohmiller of NEWH kept me in the public eye during the writing of this book. Karen McGrath and Wendy Way, who urged me on to actually finish the book. Michael Weis, good friend and colleague, gave me positive vibes while reading a chapter or two. And, of course, my sons, Alex and Christopher, and my stepdaughters, Katie and Samantha, who were present at several of the interviews and gave more than just their time and photographic instincts. Each of them sacrificed in their own unique way so I could follow my environmental quest. And there are plenty more who contributed. Finally, my partner, my Dulcinea, Maryann Mahood, who has lifted me in every way possible as a wife, as a friend, and as a believer in me.

Foreword

The original manuscript of this book was written before November 8, 2016, and written with the intent of divorcing my or others' political beliefs from science. As environmentalists of greater renown than I state often: what we feel about science is irrelevant because it doesn't change it. Any attempt to hide, defer, deny, rewrite, or erode scientific data is dangerous for any modern society, and we've recently been reminded of this. Without scientific discoveries, we might still be leeching blood to cure fevers, using shock treatment to prevent homosexuality, and praying to Roman gods that the sun would rise in the morning. It's perfectly evident that environmental conservation is in the large hands of one species alone. Federal regulations may not bring us all together politically but when stuck in the Holland Tunnel in the wake of Superstorm Sandy, we aren't exactly exchanging voter identification cards. The intensity of the Sandys of the future will cripple our economy if we don't treat this runaway planetary fever. It is a dangerous political retrograde movement to mimic Reagan-era environmental policies. The stakes are much higher in 2017 than they were in 1980. And, they were high then.

Allowing fossil fuel companies to have an active legislative role in government is not only inappropriate, it is a one-way ticket to environmental chaos. I, and others, have made the comparison of the top executives of the energy giants—Chevron, Exxon Mobil, BP, Royal Dutch Shell, and Conoco Phillips—to the tobacco company executives in the 1990s who were forced to admit that they'd been hiding science from their consumers (and nonconsumers) for decades. Nowadays, no one questions that nicotine is addictive and that tobacco-related deaths are a result of this addiction, which causes more than six million deaths per year.[1] But to know that nearly as many people in the world die annually from air pollution as from tobacco means that fossil fuel companies are as complicit in the destruction of human lives as tobacco companies have been for centuries.[2] Why are we now letting them wield such power in our government when we never let tobacco companies have that much political power?

The elimination of environmental education, conservation, and research programs is a dastardly measure to keep us in the headlock of fossil fuel companies for decades to come until they are forced to show up in Congress with their tails between their legs just like the tobacco companies did in the 1990s. Consequently, I've never seen so much environmental activism by an overwhelming majority these past couple of months. I've had good-intentioned friends and associates make the effort to console me with every move the Trump administration or the Koch Brothers make to whittle away any government role in protecting the environment and studying climate change. Notwithstanding the fact that we're all in the same boat or on the same planet, these efforts are a clear sign. People are paying attention and a concerted resistance is building. I saw it marching in New York City days after the 2016 election and in Boston at the Women's March and at the March for Science.

And more than ever, one's vote does count. So, go vote, and remember next time to vote for Her protection as well. We'll find out sooner or later that Her fever is ours too. Or as my sign in Boston said: *Make America Cool Again—Stop Burning Fossil Fuels!*

May, 2017

Introduction

Hope is what drives us all to look beyond, and faith and dreams are the brightest stars in the constellation of hope. Preserving the environment, this living and breathing apparatus that sustains life, for my children and for all future generations, is my dream. Knowing that there are passionate authors, educators, environmentalists, and people everywhere who share this dream is the basis of my faith. Faith and dreams alone won't make freshwater free or clean air communal; they won't keep ice on the ground or cool our atmospheric coils. They won't repaint our reefs or restock our streams; they aren't the science-based solutions to the environmental challenges of our times. But faith and dreams are often what unite us, and it will require a cooperative effort to solve these challenges. Somewhere deep within the spirit of collaboration is that spark that fuels my hope.

In 2002, I was giving a talk about sustainable furnishings and the impact of products on the environment. I finished the opening statement with the line "One green deed spawns another." It was meant to get the audience more broadly engaged in the welfare of our environment; the thought that a single effort might compel someone else to act seemed so simple. For thirteen years, I have closed many other talks with those same five words. If you polled 100 people about whether they wanted to preserve the planet for future generations, you'd get almost unanimously positive replies (there's always a contrarian in every crowd). Yet, here we are facing an ecological crisis without a united effort to combat it. Green deeds are being enacted minute by minute, daily, annually, and for lifetimes. Not only do we not get to witness all of them, we rarely get to hear about them. I decided I wanted to query some of my heroes who've inspired me over the years with their wisdom and commitment to greening our planet, about their one green deed. Sharing green deeds is not only inspiring, it is unifying; perhaps within this collection of engaging ideas are answers for the road ahead.

This book is twofold in origin: the unusual path I followed to become environmentally active brought me in contact with some exceptional individuals. Some are as well-known as celebrities; others have flown under the radar. All of them have equally distinctive stories that have inspired me and influenced my philosophy on our relationship to our habitat and fellow species. This book is a compilation of these poignant moments with my environmental heroes and friends and their insightful ideas, and a tribute to the spirit of Earth's active stewards.

Meeting an individual who has been a source of my environmental stimulus and wonder can be a moment of exhilaration or disillusionment. We don't want our heroes to fall short of our expectations and our reverence isn't always based on reality. Dr. George M. Woodwell, ecologist and scientist, founder of Woods Hole Research Center, made me feel comfortable from the first instant I met him. The campus and headquarters for WHRC is a testament to sustainable buildings, built at a time when few truly existed. In a frenzy of frustration with wood certification policies affecting the commercial furniture industry, I called Katie Fernholz, Executive Director of Dovetail Partners. Not only did she patiently assuage my concerns, her generosity made an industry friend of me for life. I've reveled in my pub chats with Tom Herlihy, a family friend, whom I've known since I was twelve. His vast and inventive mind created Worm Power, a successful vermicomposting farm operation, which is now helping people all over the country with organic farming practices through the hard work of millions of red worms. Hearing Frances Moore Lappé read from her book *EcoMind* on stage at Colby College, accompanied by the rhythmic sounds of a reggae band, was beyond creative. Barbara Filippone has been a David taking on the Goliaths of the seed, fiber, and fabric industries for most of her life, while tutoring me along the way. Meeting Jean Beasley, sea turtle matron and caretaker, so many years ago was more than an awakening of the spirit. In her midst, sea turtles were safe; she wouldn't ever give up, and they might just have a chance. I've met some amazing, tireless advocates for sustainability and environmental preservation over the years. Their influence helped feed my environmental passion and change the arc of my life.

In 2013, I decided I wanted to retrace my steps and reach back out to these unique people and seek their input on solutions to our environmental challenges. And, it was a personal quest to have each of them reply to the same question: if you had one green deed you'd like to see heeded, adopted, and passed on, what would it be and why? Armed with an iPad and an inquisitive mind, I set out on a mission to hear from them again.

David Mahood, 2015

One Green Deed

I t might be helpful to begin by setting the stage for what is happening to our ever-orbiting home called Earth, as well as how this came to have such a profound effect on me. Most scientists who have analyzed the data surrounding man-made impact on our biosphere indicate that we are heading into unprecedented times. As scientists, they are typically reluctant to render definitive conclusions without data to support the theory of anthropogenic changes to our life support system. As a nonscientist, relying on a practical basis for my opinion that we are dangerously altering the course of humanity, I've been shaped in part by my readings, my attendance at green lectures, and my own real observations, and I have no such reluctance. I believe my motivation is like any parent who wants a better life for their children and for those to come, so, to me, erring by scale of environmental degradation is still erring.

Having spent much of my early career in the commercial furnishings industry, I had the opportunity to work in and visit a number of wood furniture manufacturing plants. Most of these were energy intensive, wasteful, and potentially toxic. Not only was I unaware and unmoved by the impact of industrial production on the environment, I was blind to its interrelation. I was always fascinated by nature and fellow species but as a recent college graduate with degrees in Spanish and international relations selling high-end commercial furniture, I was far from an ardent ecologist. To be clear, I have nothing but respect for the craftsmen I watched steam-bend, carve, and shape wood and cut and upholster chairs. I remain a fan of the use of certified wood for furniture production and lament the outsourcing of many skilled crafts in the furniture industry. By 1997 I had spent over a decade in the industry and was at a crossroads. I was struggling to reconcile my growing concerns for the environment and my chosen career; I couldn't fathom another year unlinked to the environmental movement. This experience was in stark contrast to that of the environmentalists I had been researching from books and articles since the mid 1990s. Ultimately, I decided to create a seating and table manufacturer with a more benign relationship between manufacturing and ecology. Girded by my unscientific college degrees and my limited start-up capital, I launched Olive Designs in 1998. With little precedent for green manufacturing, I relied on my comprehension of triple bottom line principles—people, planet, and profit—as guidance. It required a great deal of creativity to reinvent some of the staples of the furniture industry like, well... staples. Or polyurethane foam, solvent-based glues and finishes, virgin plastic and glass, synthetic fabrics, undocumented hardwoods, chrome plating, and other commonly used materials and practices. This quixotic journey became the foundation of my green manufacturing education and the genesis of my transition to environmentalism. Unwittingly, our company also became a very early provider of green manufacturing education. My grasp of what was happening with our planet and its inhabitants led me to that career decision, and to the belief that its time had come. The challenge turned out to be capturing the attention of consumers who had never made the connection. By the turn of the millennium, the green furnishings industry looked very different. Today the original and emerging domestic furniture makers are much more in step with the environment community. Naively, I'd like to think I had something to do with that.

Hundreds of years ago, our planet was in ecological balance, following a cyclical pattern established over millennia. However, as the human population has grown into the billions, our ability to superconsume natural resources has also grown. This, very simply, has altered that cyclical pattern. We are currently conducting a unique experiment on the only known habitat that can support life—unique in an alarming sort of way. Not all of this has been done with ill intent or by some nefarious laboratory egghead, because, as we know, species evolve and populations grow exponentially if unchecked. It certainly takes a lot more to support seven billion people than it did for the one billion who existed in 1800. And we aren't exactly roaming the planet like Cro-Magnons surviving on the bare roots of what the land provides. We have drilled, spilled, mined, fished, dredged, burned, exploded, clear-cut, gassed, and gouged our way here. While we have also made colossal achievements as a species (our big-brained ancestors would be awed by our evolution), it doesn't change the fact that we now need to rechart our course. How we got here is not worth debating; how we react and reconstruct a habitat for generations to come is what matters.

The year 2013 is a good starting point for all of us to make a mental note. I challenge anyone in the United States to deny that they haven't been affected by a recent weather-related crisis. Whether you care to believe that these are connected to record greenhouse gas emission levels is irrelevant because we are now experiencing environmental catastrophes on a regular schedule and these events are no longer random. While climate science is based on much longer cycles, consider the extreme events that climatic activity brought about in 2013 and 2014 alone:

* Orlando and West Palm Beach set records for low temperatures on May 28, 2013.[1]
* The Black Forest Fire in Colorado in 2013 was the worst ever in the history of Colorado, burning 14,000 acres of land.[2]
* The Rim Fire in the Sierra Nevada Mountains in California burned for two months over the summer of 2013 and became the third largest wildfire ever in a state increasingly ravaged by wildfires and drought.[3]
* The widest tornado ever recorded, reaching a width of 2.6 miles, touched down near El Reno, Oklahoma, in 2013.[4]
* In 2013, California experienced its worst drought ever statewide and its highest temperature ever for the month of June in Death Valley, a whopping 129 degrees Fahrenheit.[5]
* The year 2014 set monthly records for airline cancellations due to weather.[6]
* An EF2 tornado with winds of 120 mph touched down in Revere, Massachusetts, just miles north of the city of Boston on July 28, 2014, representing the strongest tornado to ever hit the city.[7]
* New York State set the official twenty-four-hour precipitation record for the state on August 12–13, 2014, with 13.5 inches of rain at Islip, NY eclipsing the old one-day record, set in 2011, by a full 2 inches.[8]
* Phoenix, Arizona, set a new record for rainfall in a calendar day on September 8, 2014, with over five inches of rain reported in several areas of the state due to effects of Hurricane Norbert.[9]
* On November 19 and 20, 2014, lake effect brought sixty inches of snow in suburbs of Buffalo, New York, rivaling the worst snowstorm since 1977.[10]

These critical events are history, and intensified climatic activity is the common thread with each of them. While global climate change has an abundance of unpleasant consequences, in addition to the above, none of which I'm eager to witness, I have been fortunate to be in the company of amazing environmentalists from a range of disciplines who have proffered their wisdom and service to combating this global issue in their own unique way. Knowing that these stewards of the planet, and countless others, are actively influencing today's youth makes me optimistic about the future. To see young, fertile minds embracing the challenges that past generations have wrought upon them is thoroughly heartening. And I see it daily.

Earth was never our dominion to do with what we please. Our brains may have evolved greater than any other species—sometimes I question this fact in casinos and at clubs, in retail stores and on roadways, at sporting events and on social media—but that doesn't mean we were granted the right to inhibit the evolution of others. Natural selection is a moot biological theory if one species strips our planet of its rich diversity. We, the conquering heroes, must begin to reconstruct our habitat in a way that supports the restoration of the planet we once knew as nomadic hunters and gatherers.

So, to share my journey and the incredible people who shaped it to a curious new generation of Earth's stewards: one green deed spawns another.

"They can't imagine that there could be a new age that was even more attractive than the fossil fuel age can be, and will be."

Dr. George M. Woodwell

World Renowned Ecologist

Scientist

Woods Hole Research Center

I n 2002, Maryann, my girlfriend (now wife) and business partner, and I met with the interior furnishings committee for an impressive new green building design that would become the Woods Hole Research Center (WHRC) headquarters in Falmouth, Massachusetts, now called the George M. Woodwell Building. As the owner of a fledgling commercial seating and table company, the idea of providing furniture for a William McDonough-designed building for a global research organization was a thrilling experience. That day when we met at one of the original facilities of WHRC in the majestic little town of Woods Hole, Massachusetts, we were not deep into our meeting when in walked Dr. Woodwell, full of vim and vigor. We were graciously introduced to him, and he made us feel perfectly welcome. From that day on, Woods Hole Research Center became a friendly place to us.

The WHRC's furnishings committee included Katharine Woodwell, the Center's administrator and George's wife, as well as Michael Ernst, who was in charge of information technology for WHRC, and is still today. The experience was unique in so many ways. First, few companies in 2002 placed sustainability that high in priority and even fewer had compiled a list of pertinent questions for their potential vendors. I imagine for most of these vendors it must have been an intimidating experience—for me it was serendipity. My transformation from furniture salesperson to environmental enthusiast had been blossoming since 1996. Incorporating sustainability into furnishings was my primary purpose in founding Olive Designs in 1998. It was my means of reconciling my budding ecological passion with my chosen career. I truly didn't know back then that what I'd conceived as a company was one of the early adopters of sustainable manufacturing principles. The furnishings committee at WHRC did let me know however. They gave us every possible opportunity to incorporate our furniture into their design including an order for a custom glass top conference table. They even enhanced their list of questions for their vendors based on that meeting. This chapter might not have taken place if not for the support I received from Michael Ernst of that committee so this chapter is also dedicated to his goodwill and friendship.

Interview—2014

George M. Woodwell is an inspiration to many of us. At eighty-six, not only does he remain active and sharp as ever, but his passion for environmental justice representing the scientific community spans generations and puts him in very select company. Scientific research is a noble pursuit by any means but the commitment to fight political and corporate influence on climate science is not typical in the scientific community. There aren't many students of botany, ecology, or environmental law who haven't read one of his hundreds of articles or one of his numerous authored or coauthored books. His early research efforts overlapped with the publication of Rachel Carson's *Silent Spring* and the subsequent ban of DDT, and he was one of a small group of scientists who testified against its use. He has joined in founding and served on the boards of the Environmental Defense Fund, the Natural Resources Defense Council, and the World Resources Institute. He has been awarded environmental prizes including the 1996 Heinz Environmental Prize, the 2000 John H. Chafee Excellence in Environmental Affairs, and the 2001 Volvo Environment Prize. Dr. Woodwell founded WHRC after successful careers as a senior scientist at Brookhaven National Laboratory and the Marine Biological Laboratory. Frankly, I have to condense his distinguished scientific career since it alone could fill an entire chapter.

I take great pride in the fact that our products look splendid after more than a decade at the Center. Commercial furnishings, especially in lobby or conference settings, don't typically last decades. Meeting up with Dr. Woodwell again after all these years was a treat for that reason as well. It reaffirmed why I started the business in 1998, and it pinpoints a significant mark on my environmental timeline. I created a tagline for Olive Designs that used the phrase "for the undiminished experience of tomorrow." If we are compromising the experience of future generations, then we are guilty of diminishing it. Dr. Woodwell calls it "biotic impoverishment." Without healthy plants and animals, a habitat is in jeopardy of collapse. I can't say I'd ever seen a similar tagline in the commercial furniture industry but as I say now, there just weren't enough Woods Hole Research Centers to keep Olive Designs afloat.

I emailed Dr. Woodwell a few times to garner his interest in being a part of my book and to meet again at WHRC. I knew in advance that his wisdom would be worthy of sharing with anyone who might listen. One green deed could begin and end with Dr. George M. Woodwell's advice.

David: I've done a lot of talks, primarily about commercial furnishings. I started ending each of these discussions with the phrase *one green deed spawns another*. Simplistic, but the idea is if you do something, maybe somebody else will find that fascinating or it might inspire them to do something and pass it on. The goal was to have a range of people discuss this, their one green deed, what would it be and why? Interestingly enough I was looking at the NRDC [Natural Resources Defense Council] site, I think, and your quote about what people can do. It says, "It's important for people to understand the complexity of the challenge. It's going to take coordinated action, mutual respect, and life by the Golden Rule to establish a circumstance where people can live in a finite world and enjoy expanding influence on their lives and environment."[1]

George: I don't know where I said that but [laughs] that sounds about right.

David: It's a great quote. If there were one green deed you'd like to have heeded and passed on for future generations, what might that be?

George: Two levels I suppose we can think about. One of them is a global level, and obviously at the global level the first thing is to get rid of fossil fuels immediately, fast as we can. And that is one thing that's big right now. But at the same time, we have to get rid of all these toxins that you're talking about, the industrial toxification of the Earth. Those are really big issues. I suppose if you read Tom Friedman [Pulitzer Prize–winning author and *New York Times* columnist] today, it will turn out—did you read his article today?

David: No, I didn't.

George: He points to the fact that in the Middle East at the moment the various factions are pulling in different directions. He observes that ecologists insist that within the valleys of the Tigris and Euphrates, the important issue is preservation of the rivers, the land, and the agricultural potential of the region. And it really doesn't matter whether you're Sunni Muslim or Shiite or Christian if you're going to lose the whole game, everything in an environmental catastrophe, as you are, if you continue squabbling.[2] That's true in the Middle East and it is true of the world. So, one would hope that there would be a way that we could work things out in the world so that we don't wreck it for all of us. I observe that we have always had, in every government and every religion, a basis for a general agreement, a Golden Rule—that we do unto others as we would have them do unto us. And it's been forever. It has been in our religious systems and has become part of our legal systems. Lawyers call it *sic utere*—"thus to use." *Sic utere tuo ut alienum non laedas* [laughs]. But that's a good thought, and if one can build systems, governmental systems, that recognize that central principle, and then live by it, why, we have a way of managing all of these environmental issues.

Your point about one green deed flows in the same context. Before I came here I was reading board notes for the NRDC's meeting, which comes up in a couple of hours. They have a quote from *Financial Times* covering the NRDC's decision that they, the NRDC, had to look into divesting the NRDC's substantial operating reserves from fossil fuels, fossil fuel interests, because we have to match our financial support with our intellectual and political, environmental vision. And they have decided that there is no way of doing that except to set up an independent mutual fund. They decided if they're going to do that for the NRDC, they should do it for the world in general. So they went after Black Rock and FTSE [Financial Times Stock Exchange] in Britain. They have set up a mutual fund, which they are opening to university endowments and pension funds. They've done all the research and it looks attractive. The *Financial Times* wrote an article, and it was pretty clear that they figured this was an important move.[3] There is, after all, something of the order of half a trillion dollars or more in investments in fossil fuel production. One small step of the NRDC is producing reverberations elsewhere. Pretty soon we'll have stranded investments in oil, a circumstance that might be the very best change the world could see at the moment.

David: I think part of the frustration that a lot of us have is that we see that corporate America is lagging behind in a lot of ways and sometimes I feel we can't trust them. A lot of chemical companies—not all, but certainly some—are pushing back on regulation, pulling the legs out from under the EPA [Environmental Protection Agency]. And in our industry [furnishings], there are some pretty good-sized chemical companies that control things like polyurethane foam, fire retardants, and things like that

that are still standards in our industry. Your chairs don't have them [fire retardants] by the way.

George: I should put a sign on them.

David: Feel free. Well, we still had the foam issue. The foam you have is rebond—essentially recycled foam.

George: You know, we've got to renew all that. It's so important, it really is important. People don't realize that everything in this building has a story behind it. That sort of story and it's great. It's really great.

David: We were pleased because our little company had a primary spot in this building, and the fact that it still looks good today is fantastic. Even the front legs on those chairs are scrap boiler tubes. You wouldn't know it, but they are.

George: [laughs] We ought to get you to write a little essay about that chair. If you sit down in the chair, you ought to have to read the essay.

David: [laughs] Sure.

David: You're so keenly aware of what it took to ban DDT [a widely used organochloride insecticide] and the battle that you went through with it. Here we are with CO_2 parts per million exceeding 400 regularly now, which is unprecedented in modern times. What's it going to take for us, this generation, to fight this battle and win this battle?

George: Three hundred [parts per million], you got to get to 300. Better cool the Arctic. Being too modest for saying 350, he [Bill McKibben, noted environmental writer and activist, cofounder of 350.org] apologized but he goes on. He's right, if you get to 350 you can get to 300. It will take a century to get back to 300 but we should do it. It has to be the objective. McKibben can say 350 and get away with it but the NRDC won't say 350. Thinking about that, if they were to say 350 or say what I say, which is 300 and start now, they say well we wouldn't be in the conversation. We'd be immediately marginalized, and to be effective in government we must be actively talking with the participants, whoever they are. And I say, of course, change the conversation.

David: With seemingly no bottling or tabling off in the near future, it seems to me that the latest results, IPCC's [Intergovernmental Panel on Climate Change] recent results, indicate that it's drastic reduction now that needs to take place.[4] At one point, maybe in the late 1970s when energy usage and some of that was looked at, there was a reasonable measure that might have been adopted. Today, most people would say it's too late.

George: Well it's true, it sounds unreasonable. Of course, the IPCC has recently said well let's stay within two degrees [Earth's temperature]. There's no basis at all for saying that two degrees is safe. It's not safe, absolutely, not safe. What we have at the moment, which is eight-tenths of a degree, is not safe. Further, to say that we need to set a goal of two degrees is ludicrous. How those scientists got hoodwinked into that compromise, I can't imagine. It's totally outrageous and shouldn't have been done. It diminishes the power of the institution when they make a political and economic compromise like that and call it out through the mouths of scientists. "Scientific," it ain't.

David: Well, certainly you've been able to remain active and be an activist as well as being a scientist. There are scientists who are reluctant to get very active. They don't like to hypothesize [about climate change], of course. How difficult has it been for you to be at the forefront, stay active, and still be fighting the battle?

George: Oh, well, I have my critics. There are many who are critical who say scientists can't take positions. It's absurd; you spend your life working away into a position where you can predict what's going to happen and then you're required to sit back and watch it happen and do nothing about it. It's absolutely ludicrous. Of course you do something about it. That's what information is for—to use. That's what scientists are involved in producing: information and insights. At the moment, you have to use the best information you have for making judgments about the best things you can do at the moment to set the world straight. And that's what you do, which is what we all do, to sit around and say, shouldn't do that, to sit in a room and pull the shade down is useless. We go from one ludicrous statement to another ludicrous statement.

David: That leads us to the thought knowing that science has certainly been irrefutable when it comes to climate change, and we understand what's causing where we are with carbon dioxide emissions. Why are we still debating it in the public? People debating whether climate change is upon us? There's clearly political opposition to it. Even in my little world, my talks that I give, there are still people who don't want to hear about it. They still don't make the connection. How can there still be climate debaters out there?

George: There really are people who don't understand it but they're becoming fewer and fewer. There are many, of course, who see a financial advantage in continuing what we're doing at the moment. They are part of the fossil fuel age and they don't want to leave that age. They can't imagine that there could be a new age that was even more attractive than the fossil fuel age can be, and will be, if we have our way and are sensible about it; we can make a terrible mess if we don't. A terrible mess, absolutely devastating mess. It can be the end of this civilization. It could easily happen as you can see. We have people migrating now from Central Africa where it's no longer possible to carry on any sort of agriculture; it's simply too dry. You can't make a living there and you have to go somewhere where you can. There are many who want to get into Europe, and so yesterday's paper had an article about how Italy was turning back thousands of people a week, trying to get across to Sicily from North Africa. A great hegira, but that's going on of course through Spain, through the Canary Islands, not just Sicily and Italy, and also through the Balkans across Turkey, any way they can get into Russia or Balkan states. I suppose if I were an African and displaced from lands where I couldn't live, I'd be looking for a refuge too. There are droughts in every continent. We have our own in the Southwest, as you know. California's Central Valley is drying up. Mexico is dry and drying up, and people are migrating from Mexico into the U.S. at higher and higher rates. Central China has its own drought and facing the possibility of real dust storms. Australia is hotter than it's ever been; some parts of Australia are really marginally habitable. Habitable around the edges anyway and now it's hotter and getting less habitable and so on.

David: I know also that you've been very involved in the research behind reforestation and the importance of reforestation. I had the chance to be in Borneo in 2008. I visited Samboja Lestari, which is a reforestation and orangutan rehabilitation program. I know in the past you had given some idea of how much the planet needs to be reforested. Maybe you could talk a little bit about the importance of reforestation.

George: Well, we have to solve the climatic disruption problem. Roughly a fifth through a quarter of that involves biotic causes and effects. The total release of carbon into the atmosphere currently is ten or eleven billion tons a year. Between one and two of those ten to eleven billion are from global deforestation. That's 10% or more of the carbon flowing into the atmosphere annually. And it should be stopped. It's a loss of primary forests, which are one of the world's great resources in that the forests, standing, contribute to the stability of the biosphere. That's very important. At the same time, if we could reforest lands, replace forest in places that are normally naturally forested but have been deforested—Borneo, for instance, is a good example. We can store additional carbon in restored natural forests at the rate of a billion tons per million square kilometers. We can find one to two million square kilometers available for reforestation, and we shall have accounted for two to three billion tons of the total emissions. The annual accumulation in the atmosphere is not the full amount of the emissions. Sinks, including existing forests and the oceans, absorb about half of the emissions or more, leaving an annual accumulation of four to five billion tons. Stabilization would require removal of four to five billion tons of carbon from emissions in one year. The sinks in that year would continue and, for the moment, the atmosphere would be stable. Clearly, managing forests and other terrestrial vegetation is essential. But removing fossil fuel carbon is also essential, starting immediately.

David: The idea that in Borneo that there could be such a thing as ecotourism—a program where they're really valuing a standing forest instead of cutting and burning, which is where a lot of it goes—is a great thing. It was very interesting because here I am in this eco-lodge, a long way from home, and I paid the same amount as I would have for a hotel room in downtown Boston.

George: Wow, that's a good amount.

David: It is. And to think that they could ask that and that someone would pay it because they see not only the value of the reforestation program but the rehabilitation program for the orangutans. For me, it was certainly worth whatever I could pay to be there at the time.

George: What you really want to do is stop the expansion of the palm oil business. Of course that's an industrial undertaking and palm oil is really worth a lot of money.

David: I think Indonesia produces about half of the world's palm oil production or thereabouts.

George: As an industrial product [palm oil], it's hard to say you can't do that. On the other hand, you have to say, at some point, that human intrusion into the function of the Earth has to be restricted. And that's part of it right there, a big part of it.

David: You know what's interesting to me is that people, including you, who I've had the good fortune to meet one way or the other, have been very giving with time and information—I can't imagine the number of articles you've written over the years.

George: [laughs] As many as I should?

David: I really thank you for spending the time with me and being this generous. It means a lot to me.

George: I think you should defend the printed word. I'm really troubled that the printed word is disappearing. To go back to the NRDC, they have a very good journal called *onEarth*. It's been an excellent journal. It's just brilliantly done. Every issue has had a prize article in it on nature. They're ceasing printed publication to only electronic, I won't see it. It won't be sitting on the shelf; it won't be sitting on the table where I can pick it up and read it. That's absurd. We've got to defend the printed word. I've got to give them [NRDC] a lecture today. I also want to see them [written publications] on the shelf. I want to pull them off the shelf every once in a while. I remember going as a graduate student into the library and finding all these books by various ecologists all lined up and seeing all these great names and how important they were. And the titles in that particular period of time defined the great issues.

David: And you're coming up on 30 years of founding WHRC.

George: Yes, in 1985 I started the Woods Hole Research Center. Isn't it amazing? Time goes just like that [snaps his finger]. Just like that.

CHAPTER 3

"It was a very healing thing for me too to turn a negative around to a positive, give it a different meaning."

Photo courtesy of Tasi Cafe

Elaine Ireland

Indoor Toxicity Educator

Multiple Chemical Sensitivity

GreenSage

I n 2000, I was introduced to one of the more intriguing persons I had ever met in the commercial furnishings industry, Elaine Ireland. We at Olive Designs were contemplating the prospect of marketing products at the NeoCon annual contract furniture show in Chicago. It was a significant tradeshow, and the expense of exhibiting was fairly daunting to a small start-up furniture manufacturer. Elaine had similar challenges as a new green research, education, materials, and furnishings resource. Her company, GreenSage, was as much of a pioneer in sustainability as was Olive Designs. Shortly after our first meeting, Elaine suggested we share costs and coexhibit. Ours was a synergistic partnership due to our distinct services and products. Elaine's experience was unlike anyone else's that I'd known. Her commitment to sustainability ran deep. In her soft-spoken manner, she was a formidable advocate for improving indoor air quality; and not only was she a powerful presence, but she was also a patient—a sufferer of indoor chemical toxicity. She had been battling environmental illness caused by rampant indoor emissions she had inhaled for years working in newly constructed buildings as an artist, designer, and painter. At that time, VOC [volatile organic compounds] emissions were mostly unfiltered, and chemical sensitivities to humans were undiagnosed. I had heard of Legionnaires' disease, which was caused by soil or- water-borne bacteria that infected people through the air-conditioning system, but I was unfamiliar with acute indoor chemical toxicity. Hearing Elaine explain to me that she would always be susceptible to indoor air quality issues, and that her life would never be the same as a result, was equally alarming and sad. It forever changed how I view interior products in general. True to her character, Elaine became a highly informed, proud, and independent voice for greening our interiors and lifestyles. She never expressed profound anger or woe; she exemplified the true spirit of sustainability—one of caring for others and of sharing one's wisdom.

GreenSage.com became the prime and most reliable website for natural products, green building, and sustainable living. Most importantly, it was also a learning center and an outlet for Elaine to share her experience with the public. She created an e-newsletter, which included objective, well-written articles, many of which she penned herself, that was held in very high regard and that firmly established her as an invaluable resource for sustainable interiors. The Sage Learning Center was an online treasure trove of books, articles, and ultimately continuing education credits for designers seeking additional green education. Elaine's background in design proved to be invaluable to young designers entering into the field of interiors, who, at that time, had limited sources for information. In 1999, the concept of sustainable interiors was poorly defined. USGBC (U.S. Green Building Council) was pretty well established by the turn of the millennium, but they were yet to unveil the green building parameters that would ultimately become LEED (Leadership for Energy and Environmental Design), the language for green building construction and renovation for the indefinite future. In 2014, by anyone's definition, USGBC and LEED have proven to be enormous successes but back in the late 1990s, the sources for green interiors were few. LEED didn't address interior products until some years later. We at Olive Designs, one of the few green manufacturers that preceded LEED, relied on many sustainable concepts like triple bottom line principles. Elaine had been thinking about greening interiors for longer than anyone I had known. Throughout all of this, Elaine and I developed a mutual trust, and Green-Sage.com listed several Olive Designs' products as well as EnviroTextiles' hemp fabrics (Chapter 12) on their site. GreenSage was truly a pioneer of green interiors' education and Elaine, more than most, deserves her time in the sun.

Interview—2014

I had known for a few years that Elaine had relocated her business to Columbus, Ohio. Her move had more to do with her desire to be near family than anything else, but it was a significant change in scenery from San Francisco. I had lost touch with her since my career focus shifted more toward the hospitality furnishings market and since Olive Designs ceased manufacturing operations. But I never forgot Elaine. The chance to reconnect and have her share her one green deed was essential to my journey. I was as thrilled to get her positive reply as she was surprised to hear from me. In characteristic

Elaine Ireland style, she not only agreed to take part in my book but took the time to reflect on the importance of passing wisdom and education on to the next generation, or paying it forward, as it is oft-referred. She had effectively been doing that for almost three decades. We agreed to meet at Tasi Cafe on Pearl Street in an artistic area on the edge of downtown Columbus called the Short North District. I had to forewarn Elaine that I had suffered a severe black eye from a playful, but painful, incident at a college fraternity reunion a few days before our meeting. I am not normally cool enough to wear sunglasses inside a dark restaurant (see photo). I instantly recognized Elaine as she strolled into the restaurant. I was seated toward the back but within a few minutes we were able to use a more private table to chat. It wasn't very long before I realized why Elaine had inspired me and my journey to sustainability.

Elaine: I was always a person who, as I said, took pretty good care of myself, ate properly, and exercised and all that. In the 1980s in San Francisco, there was a big building boom going on. Under the leadership of the mayor at the time, the amazing Dianne Feinstein, it started with the city preparing for the Democratic convention held in 1984, which was pretty awesome. New buildings went up; the city got repaved. It was an exciting time. But it was a very toxic time. I worked in some of those buildings, and they weren't even quite finished. They'd come in and they'd just lay the carpet and you would have to move aside [sighs]. I started feeling funky little by little. I was a painter, a fine art painter, too. I had a fabulous loft in San Francisco with two other artists in the same building. God knows what kind of things they might have used that emitted fumes. But I had the entire top floor. One day in the late 1980s I was standing in my loft in the kitchen talking to someone and I just felt like I was sinking through the floor and I'm going, *What the hell is this?* I was young; of course I still worked, still painted—that was what I did—but I got worse and worse and worse. I visited a few doctors here and there and they had no clue. None.

I like collecting stuff and I wasn't much into purchasing brand-new furniture—mostly because I thought it was ugly—so my loft air quality seemed pretty clean and the painting room was separate. But it seemed like every time I went to work I felt worse and by the end of the day my head was completely foggy and swirling and I would have one bizarre symptom after another. You still have to work though, you know? But, it got to the point that I just couldn't do it anymore. I could barely function. I moved from my loft; I bought an old Victorian, thinking, *That's very clean*. It was over 100 years old, hadn't been remodeled a whole lot and they didn't use toxins back then, right? If they did, I thought, *They're outgassed by now*.

I started feeling a little bit better here and there but it just wasn't going anywhere. It was random. Doctors were finally getting a clue about some things that were going on because I wasn't the only person in town who was having this problem. So, I found a couple of really excellent doctors. One ended up giving me EPD shots. That stands for "enzyme potentiated desensitization" shots. They were a little experimental in this country but used in the United Kingdom for a couple of decades by then. It was a series of shots over two years to desensitize you to chemicals, food intolerances, and various toxins in the environment. It got a bit better, but you know, 1988 was a long time ago, and here we are twenty-five years or more. I still have issues.

This is something that doesn't go away in your system. You get those toxins in your body and they're there—or they just wreak havoc. But I'm not the type of person who just kind of sinks in a chair and eats bonbons and goes, woe is me—at least not for very long. And I was further inspired by the extraordinary Maya Angelou; I went to a talk she gave years ago. She came out on stage and she encapsulated my journey in three words. She started very quietly, looked around at the audience, and slowly said, "Runs. Falls. Rises." And you know, that's the story of my life. And this is the story of that journey for me. What do I have to do to rise above? That was my persistent question. What do I have to do to rise above?

A friend of mine said to me, "Well, what would happen if you just accepted what's going on with you?" But I was a fighter, I was feisty. This was way before I met you and started GreenSage. I was argumentative with him. I told him, I'm not going to accept it. I don't want it. I'm going to defeat this thing. But after the weekend thinking about it, I saw him and said, "You know what, Paul? You are so wise." He was probably twenty years younger than me and I just had to tell him, "You are so wise." I then changed my thinking and decided to accept what was going on, and I was a little better after that—certainly less stressed.

But, I ended up having to become my own doctor and lab rat. I had to figure out everything for myself because the medical industry still doesn't understand it. So what I did discover, and in those days we didn't know much about it, was the way you intake toxins: you eat them; you put them on your skin; you breathe them in. This is how it works. So, allowing them to dissipate is the only way to prevent them from accumulating more in your body—preventing overload. I eliminated almost everything that I might be sensitive to in order to prevent any more from accumulating in my system. And I realized well, I'm not the only person. People started calling me. People, I had no idea who they were, or how they even found me, saying, "I have the same problem. What did you do?" This is where the whole sharing phenomenon started in this field for me. Once the Internet came around, sharing the information became a lot more viable. I thought and talked about starting a website for a long time, and I had to ask myself, *Do I have the strength to do this?* And I decided, well you know, what else? This is what I need to really do. I'm helping people but it's one at a time now. What do I do to help a few more people who have never heard about me by the grapevine? It was a very healing thing for me too to turn a negative around to a positive, give it a different meaning. That's how and when I started GreenSage. In the beginning it was about informing people and then finding alternative products that they could bring into their homes. Of course I had to focus; I didn't want to include writing about food too much. At that time [1980] Whole Foods already existed so people had a little bit better handle on that issue. Skin products were, and they still are, problematic, but there are a lot of alternatives now. So, with my kind of background, I wanted to focus on buildings, the home, and the products that we live with and breathe. That's where it all started for me—in those buildings—and it's been quite the journey.

David: The fact you were willing to share that information and help so no one else had to go through the same thing that you did was special.

Elaine: We had a small team at the time. We called it the Sage Learning Center. Remember that? It developed into some courses for the interior design trade. Designers could take them online, get credits, and learn a little bit, and advise their clients to live a little healthier.

David: For a lot of us, we were just getting started, just getting our feet wet about sustainability, and you already had ten years of fighting this.

Elaine: Yeah, it was ten years by that time.

David: We're not making huge leaps in terms of making products healthier. What do you think about the roadblocks to green products in the marketplace?

Elaine: It all goes back to how people think. Change your thinking; change your life, right? Some people have told me nobody cares about that. Which, really, just means that they don't care and that they don't realize that many people actually do care, and many of them just don't know what to do about it. Big businesses have their own way of thinking. People get into a mind-set, and particularly if they're successful in business, they resist any type of change. I think our society is set up that way. It becomes a herd kind of thing. It's hard to go out on a limb and take that one step. People are afraid to do that. It requires being brave on some level. That's what I think is a roadblock. It takes entrepreneurial spirit and a lot of determination, and really, a lot of passion to go forward and change things. You almost have to create the industry all over again. It's a big task. It's a lot to take on. That's what I think is the roadblock. Big business will always be big business. But, they do come and go, and things are always in constant change, so there's hope.

David: That's part of my thought process with this. It seems like the more that we lose players in the market, the less opportunity for change; environmental change, product change, and the fact that we're always seemingly at the mercy of some of these very big companies and very big industries that are dictating things.

Elaine: Definitely. You know when we were educating people online like we talked about, which was a passion of mine, I ended up having to word things very, very carefully because I heard from some of those big companies. And I didn't write at all in an accusatory tone or with a hypercritical attitude—like is so popular these days. That's not my style. But I certainly did not like their threatening words and tone. They could crush me like a bug. I'm thinking, *OK, how can I still say what I need to say and at the same time not feel so threatened?* Because I had diminished energy and I'd already been through a lot of lawsuits, thank you very much, and who needs it? I think that's part of the problem too. But awareness has grown dramatically since then. I think now I'm very encouraged. There are a lot of small makers' movements going on right now. I think it's becoming more and more popular, so I'm hopeful, I'm optimistic. Being a pioneer is really hard. Being a settler is so much easier.

David: The whole idea of having a single movement, a single step that might influence others to do something and then pass that on down, is the basis for this book.

Elaine: One person can go one step and the next person can take it and go the next step.

David: Right. If there's one green deed that you'd like to see others adopt and pass on, what would it be and why?

Elaine: Such a small question [laughs].

David: [laughs] I can't do anything small, I know. My mind doesn't allow me to do it.

Elaine: I know, my mind is like that too. I'd like to go back to the way we each think. When your mind gets focused on what it is you can master in your life, what you are most passionate about, and what's going to sustain you as an individual to do something positive in that direction. That is where I would advise people to go first because not everybody is the same. And that mastery and passion will keep you fueled.

But if you have toxicity issues, maybe like mine, are concerned or are passionate about the whole toxic issue, then the one green deed I want to see more people embrace is to live as cleanly as you can and only buy products that are clean for you—and your family of course, especially kids. If your health is compromised, then what you can do is most likely compromised too, and you become a shadow of your former self. It becomes difficult to have any kind of impact because basically you're just in survival mode. If you don't support the toxicity in products by refusing to purchase them, they're not going to be made much longer. That's how you get the message to businesses. So, do one green deed: be conscious and make it a habit to buy clean, toxic-free, or as toxic-free as possible, products. There are so many out there now. People are already starting to be conscious—but I encourage people to go one step further. Find out what's in the product and make conscious decisions about it. Just don't buy any ole thing out there simply because it's cheap. We're suffering the consequences of cheap on many levels. It's not working.

David: To your point, it is our responsibility to not consume blindly.

Elaine: It *is* our responsibility.

David: You mentioned Maya Angelou as somebody who was inspiring to you. When you were younger, were there others who inspired you to get to that point where you finally said to yourself, *I'm going to rise back up and find a way to make a difference?*

Elaine: I was always pretty independent and followed my own path. I don't know that I was necessarily going in the direction of making a difference in the environmental world in my younger years. But, it was a different world then. Not quite so crucial to be green as now. I pretty much grew up not wasting much and always lived that way. Throw-away never made sense to me regardless of what others did. I mean my parents were babies of the depression so you grow up with that awareness. To that end, I was inspired by a very small thing, maybe in my early teens. I had a neighbor, a friend, whose parents built in a recycling chute from their kitchen right out to their recycling can—and they lived in the winter country. I remember thinking, *That's really interesting and different.* It was innovative of them. I always kept things like that in the back of my mind.

I was—and still am—very interested in the arts, as I mentioned. I don't know that I was influenced by one person necessarily. I think it's just who I am. I very much wanted to find how and where the ethereal and the commonplace met because as human beings, we are both. I'm very interested in the ethereal but I also live on this Earth. Instead of *ethereal,* you could equally say *spiritual, psychological, consciousness, creativity,* any of that heady stuff. How do we rise above the commonplace? So, it's a theme for me.

I'm not a big consumer. However, we are [women], by the way, two thirds of the economy in this country. And going back to your statement about being responsible, we can call the shots if there are enough of us who are making a difference, who are purchasing consciously, making things consciously—maybe even making things that have meaning.

So that was my thinking, where do the ethereal and the commonplace meet? And I wanted to make a difference in helping people think about it. Not to tell people *what* to think but to allow them to think about it with meaning, with some thoughtfulness. I used to give little talks way back in the day about it doesn't matter what you believe as long as you believe in something.

I was influenced by painters and artists more than environmentalists. And I had a lot of challenging experiences at a young age that influenced me too—I had a child young—I went to Kent State and I was there being shot at [1970 shootings at Kent State]. Life isn't forever, you may only be eighteen or twenty but life isn't forever so what are you going to do? Purposefulness started creeping in my brain at a relatively young age. In my late twenties, I worked on a large installation art project called The Dinner Party with Judy Chicago that was influential in the art world and women's studies world.[1] It too was different, challenging. I felt it was important and would make a difference. It was about the history of women's contribution to our culture over the centuries. We unearthed hundreds of women's lives and made them known well before women's study programs at any other universities I was familiar with. It's art; it's meaningful, purposeful; and it changed people's lives—and their thinking. People still talk about that piece and how meaningful it was—and is! That was more than thirty-five years ago. It traveled around the world. It's now on permanent display, I think, in Brooklyn [Elizabeth A. Sackler Center for Feminist Art at the Brooklyn Museum]. So, doing things in an attempt to make a difference is also a theme for me.

David: Some people get to a point that their commitment isn't deep enough to keep them moving forward and they give up and start somewhere else. You stuck with it a long time so your passions are obviously still there. I couldn't make a go of it with Olive Designs but GreenSage prevailed.

Elaine: Prevailed. I think it helps when you have little kids around in your family, I mean really little ones, and you say to yourself, *Oh, how come they're feeding them Twinkies after their soccer game?* You know? You have to still educate people and gently because you don't want to offend them, just encourage them toward a different direction. It's a challenge, and I don't know in our lifetimes if we'll see the whole thing change but there have been enormous changes in the amount of time we've been doing it I think. It's pretty encouraging.

David: Have you had situations where you've run into a whole collection of people that just don't want to believe? They don't believe in climate change; they don't believe their products have an impact; they don't believe their purchases make any difference. Have you found sometimes that you're in a situation where you're really up against a brick wall of opposition?

Elaine: Absolutely. But, I'm going to put it this way, my warrior inside is exhausted. So yeah, I had to take a different approach because the resistance just seemed like somewhere I didn't want to go anymore. Where a door was open, even if it was open a crack, then that was more the direction for me to head because my warrior was like, over. I wanted to lead more than fight. I don't think leading takes fighting—it's reeducating and convincing in a gentler way—and by just living it. I think if you live it and show by example, then it's really just like kids. Everyone can relate to their kids or their grandkids or somebody's kids. You lead by example. You don't say, "Clean your room" when your house is a mess. So that's the approach I've had to take.

David: I always feel for these scientists, like Dr. Woodwell, who are constantly asked to provide data that absolutely prove their hypotheses [on climate change and its consequences] as if it were a simple lab formula. We are at a point where we don't really know where this is going to go.

Elaine: There's the principle out there: the precautionary principle. That, I think, is something that we should just live by—the precautionary principle. If we do our due diligence and live in a precautionary way, then we don't have to go there. But yeah, I don't know that we're going to do that.

David: I hope this interview wasn't exhausting?

Elaine: No, it's been great. If this helps one person who may have toxic issues or who just wants to be cautious about it, then I would have done my job. Especially for kids, our world is so toxic. I don't know how some of them can just manage, honestly. How can we help them not go there? I wear my heart on my sleeve. I can't help it, I'm very empathic, relational, and then I just have to step back and go OK.

David: This is why people need to hear about you. It's important.

Elaine: Yeah, thank you for that encouragement. I may do that [continue writing on GreenSage]. I do know some people in the green movement here in Columbus, a movement that is pretty strong, catching up to the bay area [San Francisco]. Columbus is an amazing city, actually. I went to a talk by somebody who nationally advocates for the arts a couple of months ago and the mayor came, I didn't know he was going to show up. One of many things he said, something that resonated with me, was that art and beauty were so important, and that he's hiring an architect to ensure that all the public buildings are more beautiful.

David: I don't know too much about Columbus.

Elaine: Before I came here, me neither. I'd never been here so it was a big move but don't forget I come from pioneers [Elaine's ancestors arrived on the Mayflower].

CHAPTER 4

"It is a reciprocal relationship, that when you nurture the land, it nurtures you."

Photo by Maryann Mahood

Kathryn Fernholz

Trees, Certifications, and Policies,

Dovetail Partners

Trying to understand the idea of sustainably harvested wood or a "good" wood is complicated, or maybe it isn't. A decade or more ago, I read an online report written by Kathryn Fernholz of Dovetail Partners about wood certifications at a time when I was truly dismayed and confused about what constituted a "good" wood. I was never shy about picking up the phone and contacting an author regarding an article or issue. However, I had become a bit jaded about all of the green "experts" popping up everywhere around the turn of the new millennium, and rarely did I get anything from my entreaties other than a brochure or a brush-off. Despite these prior rebuffs, I chose to call Katie at her office at Dovetail Partners and got her on the first try. Not only did she give me the most complete understanding of the harvesting of North American hardwoods, she tutored me on wood certifications globally. Our company had selected maple from the Adirondacks of New York State for our Landing lounge chair knowing that it was from a well-managed forestry program and also that it did not meet the new LEED [Leadership in Energy and Environmental Design] requirements for certified wood.[1] These requirements only recognized Forest Stewardship Council-certified wood, irrespective of matters of origin or means of distribution. I did this with Katie's counsel and knowing that the frame manufacturer in North Carolina had worked hard to establish this relationship prior to my requests. In 2003, I was aware that the FSC [Forest Stewardship Council] program was the most respected wood certification program globally, and I remain today a strong advocate for it especially in environmental hotspot regions that are the storehouses for biological diversity. Katie gave me a much-needed tutorial on how to assess wood as a commercial product, and Olive Designs went forward with a superior understanding of North American hardwoods as a result. I thought so highly of Katie that I recommended her for the board of a respected organization run by my friend, Susan Inglis (see chapter 7), called Sustainable Furnishings Council. SFC has done more than any other organization since its founding to educate residential furniture manufacturers, suppliers, specifiers, and consumers about material sourcing and sustainable practices.

Interview—2014

I can't really say even now that I know Katie Fernholz all that well but I can say I'm a loyal supporter of hers and of her organization, Dovetail Partners. Katie serves as the Executive Director of Dovetail Partners—a nonprofit organization dedicated to solving many environmental crises that according to its mission statement provides authoritative information about the impacts and trade-offs of environmental decisions, including consumption choices, land use, and policy alternatives.[2]

After inviting Katie to speak at two subsequent NEWH [Network for Executive Women in Hospitality] Green Voice Conversations that I moderated, she's gained a number of other supporters too. Katie is a forester, first and foremost, but she also has a penchant for delving deep into a subject. I guess I've always felt a connection to scientists who seek philosophic answers in addition to scientific ones, and Katie personifies this in a remarkably positive way that permeates an audience.

I faithfully read the Dovetail online publications because not only do I trust Katie's judgment, I always learn something from them. I invited Katie to come to New York City in November 2014 to speak at an acclaimed tradeshow called Boutique Design New York for the NEWH Green Voice Conversations, a series of green educational talks I helped create for the NEWH Sustainable Committee in 2011. She had participated before in the same event in Las Vegas in 2012, so the NYC event was a reenactment of the first NEWH Green Conversation but it was also for the purpose of her inclusion in this book. Katie is imbued with Midwestern genuineness and someone I feel compelled to share with others not only because she refined my approach to sustainability but also because she is a window to environmental solutions and a hearkening to the times of Aldo Leopold.

David: It was many years ago that I began reading your articles on land management and certified wood sourcing. How long have you been at Dovetail?

Katie: Ten years now—how time flies.

David: I remember I was struggling with how to define what is considered a "good" wood to use for my lounge chair design. I knew that FSC-certified wood was the only thing LEED [Materials and Resources/Certified

Wood] was backing, yet there was wood certified from various states that seemed to be well managed. So that's how I got in contact with you.

Katie: That's right, I remember, and I am glad you reached out to me.

David: So maybe the first thing we could talk about is this whole maze of wood and certifications and the fact that USGBC continues to only recognize a single certification program. I think that has defined them maybe more than they want in terms of wood because like we were talking about earlier, there are other programs. To ignore them [other wood certification programs] is to go backward. Maybe what we could start with is what these certifications are, and why one is being endorsed and one is not? And for a new manufacturer just trying to get off the ground, it's confusing.

Katie: Yes, it is. I would start with yes, wood is a very confusing material and our relationship with wood is very conflicted. That's what it comes down to. We have core misperceptions and myths around wood that undermine our ability to engage with it in a confident way. Many people believe that using wood is bad—as in, bad for the environment. It's those core misunderstandings that make our environmental relationship with wood so complicated. Once you can wrap your head around the positive relationship you can have with wood and how that relates to positive impacts on forests and our environment, you can start down a path of getting through all that. But as long as you're in this point where you're in conflict with using wood because you think using wood is bad for forests, then once you're in that conflict it's easy to get into the conflict of competing certification systems and this win-lose mentality. To me, you have to back it up to the point of having a positive, empowered, clear relationship with wood so then you can sort through this. It's not this black-and-white, win-lose thing, it's a win-win thing once you really understand what you're looking at. And for me, that's why I went into forestry because I come from a farm so I grew up understanding that we rely on the land to survive for our food and so many things. But when I would travel as a kid—when we would go camping—I'd see forests and what I recognized is that we rely on that too, but it's a natural system. These are natural wild trees that give us our homes and energy and shelter and furniture and products, and it's not a cultivated system like farming. Somehow if we do things right, we can meet our needs through a natural system. That's powerful. For me then it was like *OK, that's intriguing and I want to actually go study that and understand that, know the names of the things that make up a forest, understand how trees grow, what the ecology is, how to walk through a forest and read it.* That's why I went into forestry. For people to get over an idea that using wood harms forests, we have to embrace the incredible, powerful opportunity to meet our needs through natural systems.

Oftentimes in America, we romanticize indigenous people or we romanticize Native American tribes. If we indulge that romanticism for a moment, we can think of those communities as groups as people that lived off of natural systems: woodland people. We still have the opportunity to do that today. We can be a woodland people and understand what that means. We see our woodland culture in today's wild crafting where people go out and forage for food. We see it in our hunting traditions, maple syruping, and cutting trees for the holidays. All of those kinds of trends—new and old—they are all a part of the idea of meeting needs through natural systems. That's a long-term exciting trend that once you get into that, you get into—OK, well, what is the capacity of a natural system, what can it provide, at what rate, at what yield? You get into sustainability questions that are much different than black or white, win-lose, and that's ecology, that's about interacting with your natural system in a place of love and responsibility not fear and anger and guilt. Our environmental relationship in this country is changing from that fear-based, guilt-based relationship to one of—I want to actively care for the environment—I need knowledge and tools to do that.

David: I remember when I had the lounge chair in the marketplace at the price I was charging for it, I felt that it was fair value to the wood. I felt it was a responsible way of using wood and getting value out of it because wood can be devalued. Paper is not the best use, although I realize it's a by-product, but still.

Katie: Having higher-value uses of wood is important. In parts of the world where wood is primarily used for fuel wood or cooking, there often isn't a wood industry that creates quality jobs—you need that whole spectrum. You need markets that use the by-products or the low-value materials so you can support the whole system. One of the most exciting things happening in North America right now, in other parts of the world too, in Europe and in Australia, for example, is developing cross-laminated timber and other materials to enable tall wood construction. Doing seven- to thirty-story buildings primarily with wood adds tremendous value to material. You always have to do new product and market development with some caution and make sure we're being responsible, et cetera, but having that whole spectrum from fuel wood to high-value product is what gives you a robust, forest-based economy, and that's what can drive societies that live off of forests, that live from sustainable forests. Then if you get food from a forest, maple syrup, mushrooms, or whatever, it just adds to that whole spectrum; it supports that diversity.

David: We were talking earlier about the importance of reforesting some of these areas and you were mentioning how a lot of it is basically being converted. Land conversion can be very devastating. Creating more carbon sinks is so important to the stabilization of carbon dioxide emissions. I've heard from others about creating and preserving carbon sinks. Do you think we can do that in balance with the harvesting of wood responsibly?

Katie: Oh yes, we can do anything we want. I firmly believe that either in the United States or globally if we had a clear vision of our future, we could have it. Almost every country on this globe has done amazing things when they're pushed to do it. Build the Great Wall of China or whatever. Every part of this planet has done amazing things when they have a clear vision of it.

If I just focus on the United States and the forest opportunities in the United States, right now about 72% of the land that can grow trees in the United States is growing trees. That's a testament to the fact that we can make a living in this country growing trees; we've prioritized forests within our national forest system and state forest systems, and private land owners are provided incentives to grow trees, too. So we have 72% of the land that could be growing trees, growing trees. Well, how could we get at that other 28%? Because a lot of that other land that isn't growing trees is agricultural field: corn and soybeans, et cetera. Could we modify our food system in such a way that more of that land could be put into trees? Could we add value? Could we look at agricultural systems like agroforestry or orchards that incorporate trees within highly productive food systems? I just think we can do anything. We can do anything. It's having a clear vision of what that looks like and then being committed to the investment it takes to get the kind of benefits we want from that.

One of the key things is that when we have this conversation about how forests are part of carbon storage and carbon sinks, we have to be very careful about how that relates to our use of wood products. You can imagine, if somebody said tomorrow that our best carbon sink is going to be tomatoes or that somebody looked at the science and said, "Oh my gosh, tomatoes store carbon like nobody's business." Nobody would say that we need to stop eating them. No, they would say, "How can we drive the market to grow more tomatoes?" It's so important when we think of forests as carbon sinks that we don't just look at the preservation of forests to reach our carbon goals. In cases of forests like the redwoods then yes, those trees can live for hundreds or even thousands of years and we should preserve and protect them, monitor their health, et cetera. But most of our forests need to be cared for if they're going to be carbon sinks. When we talk about the role of forests, we have to connect forests and forest products because it's that economic driver that will expand the ability of forests to store carbon.

David: Well in the twentieth century, we did some damage to our original forest cover. Some of the indigenous forests are no longer there. They're not coming back obviously because they can't. The idea is then let's look at what we're growing and let's harvest responsibly. And here in North America, we do have an advantage.

Katie: We can't undo history. As a forester, I can only tell you how many times I've said, "Oh I wish we could go back before the Homesteading Act." If you look at the history of the United States and have to pick one moment that has driven our land use—the biggest impact was the Homesteading Act, which, basically, told people to go out, clear the land, and be farmers. It said: Americans, you are farmers, go get rid of the trees and farm. If you could have just tweaked that [Homesteading Act] to say grow trees also, something besides go clear the land and farm, but we can't undo history.

David: Hopefully, we won't have another Civil War to get to that point.

Katie: [laughs] Yes, and hopefully we can learn from history, try not to repeat it too often. But I do think we know what influences land use, and it is economics. With the right economics, we can continue to use the land to grow trees and we can have all the benefits of forests. It still won't be what it was. You can't set back time.

David: I'm back to the origin of your interests in this. How did you decide at some point that you wanted to be a forester? And that you wanted to be involved in land management, because that's a life dedication.

Katie: For me it is, certainly. My identity is as a forester. That's my professional and personal sense of who I am. It came from being on a farm, loving the land, and loving that relationship with the land. That it is a reciprocal relationship, that when you nurture the land, it nurtures you. I love that. I grew up with that. But, like I said, when I interacted with forests, it amazed me how it's a natural environment. They're wild things, not cultivated, not hybrid or controlled. What's funny is the things you grow on a farm are so vulnerable. They're these plants where their fight has been bred out of them. You have to baby them, you have to fertilize them, protect them, and they don't compete well with weeds. Some of them, of course, are strong hybrids and whatever else, but they're not wild. They don't have that vibrancy of a wild plant. When you're in forests, we've all seen it, when you go hiking and you see trees growing out of rocks or from stumps, shallow soils—less than ideal conditions. It is that expression of a will to live that you experience in a forest, which is very different than a cultivated environment. A forest has this personality, this energy, this fight to it. It has this energy to it that's very different. I love being part of that. So I was always attracted to forests growing up because of its differences from a farm. I grew up on a windy, dusty, prairie farm, and you go into the woods and it's quiet and the air is clean and it has this calm sense to it, so as a kid I was always attracted to that contrast. I went in to study forestry from that love [perspective] where what I wanted was to understand it. There's that saying: to love something is the desire to understand it. For me that's what it was. I didn't go into forestry school because I wanted to be a forest ranger. No, no, I wanted to learn the names of trees, understand them, be able to listen to them, so for me being in forestry and going into the forest is like walking into a room of old friends. I go into a forest and say to myself, *Oh, there's the Douglas fir. Last time I saw you...oh, I remember seeing you in Oregon.* It's cheesy [laughs] but that's what it's like for me. I walk into a forest, especially if I go there alone, I feel I can hear and sense the energy of that forest. As a forester when I go into a forest that's been cared for, where the trees are healthy and the understory ecosystem, the biodiversity, is there, where all the pieces are working together, the energy is so much different than if you go into a forest say out West that has been neglected and is prone to fire and is dying. As a forester or anybody who's a gardener or farmer, or maybe even people that work with children in a classroom, you know this energy when you go into a healthy place and you say, "Ahh, this is good." It's not about me, it's about the health and the vibrancy of a situation. If more people could understand that forests can have that same feeling. You can go into a forest, and as a forester, every forester would say this, and it's not an arrogant thing, you can feel when a forest is asking for help. That's the way I would say it. I firmly believe everywhere on the planet, and certainly in the United States, forests evolved with people. People and the forests of this country were intimately related for thousands of years, and I firmly believe that in many situations in the United States today, the forest misses us. That when we go out into the forest—it's asking for our help. It's asking for us to care for it in a gentle, loving, nurturing way. It has gifts it wants to give us. It wants to give us food, shelter; it wants to give us energy; it wants to give us a full experience with nature, and in return it wants us to care for it. I think that is the opposite side of this fear we've been in where we think using the forest is harmful. It's moving away from that to say it wants us to care for it. If we give and we're thoughtful, careful, and humble in our interactions, it will care for us. Almost every forester I work with will tell you that same thing. They go into forestry because they love the forest and their charge, their mission, today, is to care for the forest in a way that will help it care for us. That's not a hands-off thing. In many situations, that means there are forests we need to interact with aggressively. We need to remove invasive species; we need to harvest trees so the native trees can come back; we need to reduce wildfire risks; and we need to plant. It's not this light-handed thing. It's introducing fire, it's using chainsaws, and in some instances, it's going to be using chemicals. As you know, there are weeds, diseases, and invasive plants in our forests today that we need to respond to in order to have a vibrant system.

David: They're invasive, they weren't there initially.

Katie: Right. For me I wanted to go into forestry so that I could have the tools and the information to be part of building that vibrant, healthy, happy, productive system. Because when you experience that, when you spend time in forests where people have a positive relationship, it's a powerful thing. It's a beautiful, powerful thing. I'm always amazed… we should all just be foresters [laughs]. It's such a natural thing. I always think there are more people who could be foresters.

David: It's interesting, and it makes me wonder: why aren't we all more environmentally active?

Katie: Really! Because when you tap into that part of yourself, this whole door opens. I'm not saying everybody has to be the same, but I do think there are a lot of people that if they allowed themselves to go there, they would discover amazing things.

David: Well, you know this matter about nature deprivation and nature deficit disorder with kids growing up, certainly urban kids, who don't have the benefit of that and they rarely have the opportunity to visit.[3]

Katie: You know what's interesting about that, though? There are studies that show spending time in nature, spending time outdoors, can create all kinds of health benefits and psychological benefits. They've even found that exposure to an interior [environment] with natural wood grain has very similar benefits. There's a study in the last year, coming out of Canada, that if you have an office building or a hotel or a bedroom or a home—where it's the exposed wood grain—you can measure some of those same differences in your blood pressure, in your heart rate, all these things versus sitting in a room where you're looking at nonorganic materials. To me, that's just amazing because it reminds us how connected we are. At some inner level that's how connected we are to nature. That it's our home and it misses us and we miss it and we need to spend more time together [laughs].

David: It gets into the whole concept of biophilia and biophilic design. There are a number of architects recognizing that if they build a space that preserves natural habitat with exposed views, the mood changes, and the productivity levels change—it is fascinating. The other thing to distinguish talking about healthy North American forests and then talking about rain forests, which is a very different type of preservation and usage, is that its relationship to humankind is very different. What do we do within those areas versus healthy North American forests in contrast?

Katie: It's very difficult. It's like we talked about before, if you could travel back in time to rewrite the Homestead Act and try and influence what we did to, arguably, the original or presettlement forest. If you try and travel back in time through America, you can start to imagine what the challenges would be to influence the economic drivers at that time and what we were trying to do as a nation in terms of growing. But it also opens up the idea that even what we think of as the presettlement forest in North America, it had been inhabited by people for thousands of years. So take all those lessons from America and you export that to where certain countries are today, whether it's South America or parts of Africa or Asia, we can extrapolate from that American history to what's going on in places in the world today. You have places in countries that are driven to develop economically with greater productivity, greater economic returns, and they're diverting from the indigenous cultures and the historic land uses in those regions. What's happening today in rain forests and tropical forests and other developing parts of the world is repeating history to some degree. For me, there's this whole spectrum of tools we have to apply—everything—including social programs that help support indigenous ways of life that protect that historic knowledge. Ecologists and others often talk about that in America: what if we knew what some of the Eastern tribes knew? We've lost all kinds of knowledge. There was a map that came out last year where Native American tribes collaborated to map 595 tribes that existed in North America before European settlement.[4] So there are volumes of knowledge that we've lost. When I look globally, that's one of the things for me, that social end of the spectrum, and the things that we have to do to capture or retain and support the vibrancy of cultures because that is information that's ecological knowledge—everything. On the whole other end of the spectrum with legal enforcement and economic drivers, if we are going to avoid some of the impacts that America had on its forests, then we have to go to that whole toolbox of solutions. I don't see it as... it's not a silver bullet. It's not like, well, we just have to do preserves or we just have to do legal enforcement. No, no, it's a whole spectrum in figuring out how do we sustain long-term use of this resource in a way that maintains people and forests? The most devastating thing is either permanent conversion of forest land to a developed use or high impact even if it's temporary conversion to annual cropping, which can have long-term impacts on the soil. If we look at tropical regions, there is a history of slash and burn, rotational agricultural, so we shouldn't be afraid that every time a tree is harvested that it is deforestation and that is the end of the rain forest. It's looking at: What's the right scale of land use change? What can be supported? Some level of slash and burn—temporary agricultural is historical—that's what happened in North America, too; there were plenty of times in the Eastern United States in the 1600s that areas were cleared. Therefore, we can't be afraid of cutting and land use change in the rain forest if it's part of a system, part of a game plan.

David: Native Americans were notorious for burning forests and they did it systematically.

Katie: They did it in a way where there's a method to the madness. I think that's part of what we're missing sometimes, we only see the madness. We don't necessarily understand there's a way to do this.

David: So I have to get to the question [laughs]; we've done twenty-five minutes here already, so I am posing the question, if there were one green deed you would like to see heeded, implemented, and passed on, what would you say and why?

Katie: I love this question. It's a very clear, a very, targeted question. For me, targeted questions always bring out a real strong reaction—a heartfelt one. To me, the one green deed I would wish upon everyone, of course, is to plant a tree. But that's not the end of the green deed. The green deed is to then have a relationship with that tree. You can do so many things, but to me the green thing we all need to do is commit to having a relationship with our environment, and we can start with a tree we plant. For me, where this came up, when I was still in forestry school, there was an author from Western Minnesota where I grew up, Paul Gruchow, and he wrote a book called *Grass Roots* and the subtitle might be *Story of Home* or something like that [*Grass Roots: Universe of Home*, 1995]. It was one of those books I read when I was in college; I was probably three chapters into it, and my biggest reaction was, I don't need to write a book. If I were going to write a book, Paul Gruchow already wrote the book I would have written. For me, it's a beautiful book. It's like a Western Prairie version of Aldo Leopold's *Sand County Almanac*. It's a story of home, and it resonated very strongly with me. He has a short story in there where he talks about having relationships with our natural environment. His analogy he uses is we need to get away from one-night stands where we don't even know the other person's name.[5] When we go out into nature or when we see plants in a nursery, we don't even know their names. That's an indication of how we don't have a relationship. If you don't know something or someone's name, you don't have a relationship. That's the very basic starting point. To me, the one green deed is to plant a tree, in part because trees are long-lived. They have a life potential that is more so than planting a garden. It inherently draws you into the potential for the long-term relationship. So, plant a tree and then form a committed relationship with that tree. Name it. I don't care if you call it by its scientific name. Name it Bob, I don't care [laughs]. But have a name for that tree, visit that tree, and observe that tree. Not just make it a science project where you take pictures every Monday but explore what it means to have a relationship with a long-lived plant. Just to live in that relationship, make it whatever it means personally. Dress it up for the holidays. Give it presents. Celebrate its birthday [laughs]. If we want to be green and want to support the environment, it's not just doing something and checking the box. It's that commitment; it's that relationship; it's exposing a part of one's self to that risk of loss, and to say that I'm going to plant a tree and see if it is going to be here next year. It's that relationship, it's that love. It's putting something into it besides just taking a picture, doing a ribbon cutting, and moving on with your life. It's that relationship. It's also in an Aldo Leopold quote, and I won't get it right, but something like I'm not afraid of what you will do to nature. The more time you spend with nature, I'm sure it will do wonderful things to you.[6] It's along those lines of if you just put yourself out there with nature, it will most likely be incredibly good and positive and amazing, but it is that relationship piece. I think that's so important.

David: I agree, that connection...

Katie: It's hard. I know it's hard in the world that we live in, to really take risks, to be vulnerable. There's a saying too, like I said before, that love is the desire to understand. There are many definitions of love but I always think that's an interesting one. There's also a common saying—that fear is the only real emotion and that every other emotion is a variation on fear. Another way to define love is that it's the fear of rejection, that is, fear is at the heart of love. I think that if we can wrap our heads around the emotions and not run away from the emotions that come from our environmental relationships, we'll be stronger. Because environmental challenges are scary—are we doing the right thing now for the future, for our children? They're really scary things, so we need to find a way to bring our heart into them, because you can't just deal with them in your mind. They aren't these mathematical challenges; there's an emotional element there. To me it comes from that being vulnerable—having that relationship where you can tap into the emotions—will help us make better decisions.

David: Well put. One of the things that scares me, and this is an area I don't know a lot about, among many, is my concern about the other consequences of climate change and Earth warming. For example, the migration of pests and vectors are impacting areas where they had no purpose being and hadn't been before. I imagine that's got to wreak havoc on our forests. Talking about Colorado before, I assumed that may have been one of those incidents of invasive species or maybe not. I don't know the story. Does that frighten you at all because to me that is frightening?

Katie: Yeah [nods head several times].

David: It may impact so many industries—the sap farmers up in New England are struggling, for example. What kind of challenges do you think those will be?

Katie: It is, it's very scary. Climate change, invasive species, exotic pests like emerald ash borers, Asian longhorn beetles, to name a few, and there's no shortage of invasive aquatic wildlife. It's really messy. I think for me what's the most difficult to wrap my head around is precautionary measures. How much we can stop the trade or the transport of things, because increasingly that's not realistic. The white nose syndrome that's killing our bat species is a good example. Cavers that travel around the world recreationally—you can't prevent these things. You can't quarantine everybody every time they cross the state line. The other end of the spectrum is our level of comfort with acting aggressively in response. That's very scary as well. For example, there are chemical treatments to protect ash trees from emerald ash borers that appear to work very well. I was at a working group where they were debating expanding the purchase of this chemical and expanding chemical treatment and someone in the working group said, "Well, we know it works, let's just go get all we can and do it."

And another person on the working group said, "Well, years ago, we thought DDT was a miracle as well."

That's the scary thing—there are limits to what we can do preventatively, but we also have to be cautious at how reactionary we are. We should have learned those lessons as well. Like the ecologist and the natural scientist, where I have come to, is that somewhere over multiple life spans, over the next hundred years, we have to wrap our heads around some homogenization of our environment. That some plants that thrive that are uniquely adapted are going to be widespread around the world and some diseases as well. That's hard for me to accept because I do have an attachment to the integrity of ecoregions. That's the way my mind thinks. But it's the spectrum of solutions, again; I try to step back to what's the long-term vision, or the long-term trend, and how can we live within that reality? That's what we have to figure out. The way I rationalize it, too, is that we've gone through this in the past, there have been extinction events. Perhaps not at the rate or certainly not with the same kind of causes we're seeing today. We'll need to somehow wrap our head around it and bring all of the tools to bear. The other thing that comes to mind as I look at the threats from invasives and exotics and diseases and radical rapid change to ecosystems is that in those cases I have been able to accept a role for things like genetic modification. It's hard for me to accept a modification of things just for making more money, but if there's a way that we can use technology to protect genetic diversity, then I think that might be the best use I've heard of for that type of technology. It doesn't mean I want to do it everywhere all the time. It's one of those things that technology, in and of itself, isn't good or bad, and genetic modification is a type of technology. How you use it determines whether it's good or bad. When I look at threats from aggressive diseases, that's the one place where I can say this might be the best intent for that technology. When I talk to environmental-minded people, I think that's an important conversation, because I think in the next generation we're going to be very challenged on those kinds of technologies. As environmentalists, we're going to have to figure out how to articulate good solutions, good reasonable positions with scientists on appropriate uses.

David: I think that is going to be a big challenge. There's going to be a knee-jerk reaction when you talk about genetically modified anything.

Katie: Right. Technology is powerful, and finding the right way to use it is a challenge. Every generation has to deal with that—how to appropriately use our innovation. It's just one of those things. The benefit of genetic modification is that you can be much more precise. In so much of plant-breeding technology, you may go through years, decades, of hybrids and crosses before you end up where you want to be. If we just look at the speed and the precision that genetic modification offers and use that judiciously, I think there are opportunities there.

David: I hesitate to use the word but I think there are simple ethics that have to be calculated in. I see technology sometimes running rampant without an ethical cause behind it. To modify something, like you said, for profit motives has only one purpose.

Katie: Right, exactly. To use technology in ways that have short-term gains and long-term consequences I think is what we all want to avoid. We want long-term gains in efficient ways. It also comes back to a whole idea: we have to get out of being afraid of it. We have to really commit to understanding it and having thoughtful conversations.

David: I'm glad you brought that up. That's a really interesting topic.

Katie: Anyone who spends any time with me will always tell you it's one of my core philosophies. I think the one green deed is important. If I could wish anything, there are two things I'd wish on people: I think people make terrible decisions when we're afraid. Freeze, flight, fight, whatever the saying is.[7] We make terrible decisions when we're afraid. If we could move out of fear and into a place of strength, empowerment, and love and comfort, the possibilities are just endless. I always wish that people would be less afraid and feel stronger. The other part of it is that I always wish everyone could be indoctrinated with the scientific method of exploring questions and solutions. Where you can step back and have some perspective and not methodically but systematically think through the questions and the evidence—that rational approach. We don't all have to be Mr. Spock [TV character from Star Trek]—that would probably be a very boring universe—but an element of that in the way that we approach challenges. A confident, systematic, not nonemotional, that's not my point, but a place of confidence rather than fear. That's why I'm always a big fan of STEM [science, technology, engineering and mathematics] education, women in science, and those kinds of things. For me, that's why I'm interested in those initiatives as well. Like I said, not everybody has to be Mr. Spock, but a scientifically trained populace is a powerful thing.

"I think the turtles will find a way; I think they're survivors. I hope so, I've bet my life on it."

Photo by Christopher Mahood

Jean Beasley

Sea Turtle Savior

Karen Beasley Sea Turtle Rescue and Rehabilitation Center

One of the first real altering events in my environmental journey was discovering back in the early 1990s that sea turtles were endangered and in trouble after close to a hundred million years of existence. That was disturbing to me because it was purely a strike against just one species: us. We couldn't claim that another species had displaced them or that their habitat had shrunk beyond any sustainable size. When a creature has done the same thing successfully for millions of years, a sudden decline in numbers doesn't make biologic or even evolutionary sense. Coastal development, ocean bottom trawling, motorboat mishaps, soup and egg recipes, sea-bound chemical brews, plastic jellyfish, beachfront lights, poaching, and just your basic climate change consequences prove that we as a species can unwittingly eradicate another in very short order. Sea turtles were once so abundant that they were referenced in everything from early Native American tradition to the first European explorers to coastal cities along the Atlantic Ocean to a worldwide fashion statement known as tortoiseshell. I became so fascinated with sea turtles that I named my new business, Olive Designs, after the smallest of the sea turtles: olive ridley turtles. I wanted to make more than a marketing connection like some Fortune 500 companies are guilty of doing, so I determined that I would make a donation to a sea turtle organization—using profits from each order. I made a number of calls to a variety of marine conservation organizations in 1998 and ultimately was given the name of Jean Beasley, who had recently opened up a rehabilitation center in 1997. My first call with Jean was far more than I anticipated. Beyond productive, and beyond expectation, I knew at that point I would try to support her efforts for as long as I could.

My trips to the sea turtle hospital on Topsail Island, North Carolina, were inspiring on two levels: first, anytime I could provide even the smallest of financial assistance was motivation for me to keep selling our products, and second, to witness the effort to heal and ultimately return sea turtles to the ocean was such a moving experience. Imagine if our odds of surviving to adulthood were one in a thousand.

Jean started the turtle hospital as fulfillment of her daughter's plea and example and as a result of Jean's long commitment to sea turtle conservation. She is solely funded by private donations, and through her Herculean efforts and that of her team of dedicated volunteers, the Karen Beasley Sea Turtle Rescue and Rehabilitation Center has survived hurricanes, relocations, and economic doldrums. Her story is remarkable, and I wanted everyone to know about it and be as inspired as I've been all these years later.

Interview—2015

Building and operating a volunteer-based sea turtle hospital requires a driving force of boundless passion and energy. Jean has that in spades. She makes no bones about the fact that sea turtles are her focus. Since it had been some years since I provided financial assistance for the hospital and furniture donations for the intern house that she also opened, getting in contact with Jean was a challenge. After a series of emails and the snail versions, I was fortunate to reach Terry Meyer, who has always been responsible for the turtle hospital website and now is the office manager of the hospital. I originally met Terry when I was seeking help with the Olive Designs' website. Terry is a kindhearted woman who is also an ardent advocate for sea turtle preservation. Terry intervened on my behalf, and it wasn't long thereafter that I got an email reply from Jean. We determined that we would conduct an interview once the summer visitation season had ended. Traveling to Topsail Island, North Carolina, was not a straight line for me since my rendezvous point with my sons is Greensboro, the Piedmont region of the state. Since she opened the turtle hospital, Jean Beasley has gotten well-deserved national recognition, being named Animal Planet Hero of the Year in 2007 and Ocean Hero of the Year award in 2013 by Oceana.[1] I even remember Ray Anderson (1934–2011, Founder, Interface) telling me once that he was moved by a short CNN segment on Jean and the turtle hospital that he watched while sitting in an airport. That recognition underscores my genuine appreciation for her work, for her as a person, and for my interest in sea turtle survival.

We were finally able to meet at the new KBSTRRC on Topsail Island on the twentieth of October. My youngest son, Christopher, accompanied me because we combined the interview with a college visit to University of

North Carolina at Wilmington. Christopher is in the midst of the challenging process of evaluating colleges, and he wanted to visit UNC-W. It had dawned on me that Christopher's age coincides with that of Jean's turtle hospital. In light of that fact, I brought a photo of a very young Christopher in one of the Topsail Turtle Project shirts designed by Karen Beasley—in the very same color Jean wore the day of our meeting. I had visited the sea turtle website often, and I had become aware that they were building a new and improved hospital. But, I was not prepared for what I saw at 2:30 p.m. on October 20.

David: Here we are, all these years later [laughs]. This facility is so incredible, and you deserve it obviously for all the hard work you've done.

Jean: Hard work a lot of people have done.

David: Part of the reason I wanted to come back here for this chapter in the book was because this was such an inspiration for me when I started my business. Not many people have the courage and compassion to honor someone as you have. Your dedication, you dedicating your life to sea turtles in your daughter's name and memory, is as moving a tribute as I've ever really known.

Jean: Thank you for those words.

Dave: This is an opportunity, if you can, to share some of the story behind the creation of the Karen Beasley Sea Turtle Rescue and Rehabilitation Center, which we are seeing now in its much new elevated form.

Jean: [Laughs] Who'd have ever thunk it, either.

David: Truly.

Jean: Our family, first of all, my husband and I lived here, and we were married in 1958. He just graduated from the college ROTC [Reserve Officers' Training Corps] program so he was in the Marine Corps stationed at Camp Lejeune. We fell in love with the island—never saw a sea turtle—never thought about one. Didn't even know such things existed, I don't think. Part of my story is that I vowed after high school biology that I would never cut up anything again nor would I deal with anything that was living that I was studying like that. When I got to Duke [University] and had my first conference with my advisor; it's a liberal arts school so you have to take a science. I said, "I'm not cutting up anything. Find me another science." I took botany and I worked in the Sarah P. Duke Gardens. The moral to that story is to never say what you're not going to do with your life because you don't know [laughs]. We fell in love with Topsail Island and knew even in those early days of marriage that we wanted to retire here. We started coming back immediately so our children were here every year. We started to notice the turtle tracks and wonder about them, what they were. Did some investigating but it was very difficult to learn much about them at that stage. Even in the 1970s we tried to find books on sea turtles and there was nothing. But we saw our first sea turtle nest with the mother coming out of the ocean in 1970. It was a momentous thing for our entire family. It takes her about an hour and a half when she's on the beach to find the spot and go through everything that she does to make sure it's as safe for the eggs as it can be. Most everybody went to bed, but my daughter stuck it out with me. She was right under our deck so we watched her. That's a long love affair and it certainly has been one, and it was one for her also. Karen grew up caring about the sea turtles. We didn't see hatchlings at all because our time [of the season] here was not when there would be hatchlings on the beach. We would be back getting ready for school in Ohio at the time. Karen wanted to come to school in North Carolina, and did, graduating from Wake Forest University, cum laude with a degree in communication. Still keeping that love of sea turtles, every summer we were doing something for the sea turtles. In the early days, when we saw the tracks we would call the federal number. There was like a hotline number, not just for turtles, but also for wildlife in general. We would report the tracks and sometimes nobody came and nothing was done, and sometimes somebody came in a pickup truck with a cooler and shovel. The dug up the nest, put it in a cooler, and drove off with it. At the time we didn't know any different. As we pursued more information about turtles—remember no computers then—there was no way you're googling anything. You were very dependent on doing research the hard way. As we learned more about turtles, one of the things that we learned was that turtles return to the area they were born. Anyhow, we looked at each other like *Hey, if they're taking all the eggs away they won't be coming back here.* So, we stopped calling. We'd split up and walk the beach early in the morning. Usually my husband was still working, so it would be me and the kids down here, and we would stay for a couple of months. We'd walk the beach, some of us would go one way and some of us would go the other with a broom. Wherever we saw the tracks with the turtles we would erase them; yet we would write down where it was—the nest locations. This was for a couple years from the late 1970s into the early 1980s with children growing up, et cetera, et cetera. Then in 1982 my husband was transferred to Wilmington, so we made this into our permanent home. Karen, as I said, graduated from Wake Forest still working with the turtles every summer. She became ill and was diagnosed with leukemia, ultimately. She had been working for a company for a couple of years but that was put on hold because she went through chemotherapy and some radiation due to some additional problems that developed because of the leukemia. During that time when you're interested in something, the word spreads, and then everybody tells you their experience with that thing. People started to call us and say that they were out on the beach and saw these tracks and what have you. Karen started giving these little programs about turtles. Fifty to sixty people would show up. One day when the phone was ringing off the wall and Karen was trying to get some sleep, she said, "Hey, someone needs to organize this."

I said to her, "Be my guest." So, she did. She organized the beach program, wrote its mission statement, and gave it its name: Topsail Sea Turtle Project. She recruited and trained volunteers to walk the beach to report the tracks since we couldn't do it all. She was totally immersed in that program, and it really became a life force for her over the almost five years of her illness that we thought, at times, was winning the battle. I was busy doing lots of other things, so she was running that program—I was just her assistant. When truly her sudden decline, which ended in her death, was somewhat unexpected even though we had known for a long time it was a vicious type of leukemia. She did tell me right in those final days because she had worked for a company where an insurance policy was still in effect, she said, "Mom, you know that I have an insurance policy. You are the beneficiary. If I don't make it, I want you to do something good for sea turtles with it."

After her death, that was the furthest thing from my mind. I didn't even go there. I will tell you the morning she died that later that night the phone rang at two o'clock in the morning. It was the police department from one of the towns on the island. The guy knew Karen because she was out on the beach at all hours. He said, "I know we all grieve the loss of your daughter and I hate so much to call but we got a turtle in trouble and I didn't know who else to call." I told him I'd be right there. I got up out of bed and I went, and that was what threw me right into answering that call that I couldn't avoid and couldn't ignore. I still had no thought of a hospital—never, never did that enter into either of our minds. We were just beginning to see very sick turtles and occasionally one that was barely alive that died very quickly, washing in with severe boat strikes, that kind of thing.

After Karen's death, I took over the organization to try to keep it going. Of course I wanted to for her—but still no thought for the money. We began to get more injured and sick turtles, and I learned that there was no funding to take care of them. When we would call the wildlife people and tell them, hey, this turtle is injured badly, they'd just take them out and dump them to die a slow and horrible death. It just was just not in the cards. We finally had one turtle wash up that needed to be euthanized. It was suffering so much I just couldn't see nothing being done for it. I promise every answer won't be this long or you'll be here till tomorrow [laughs]. I had to drive all the way up to the vet school to get that turtle euthanized because local veterinarians did not have permits to deal with protected species. They were very apprehensive about putting one down when they didn't have the authority. That's changed a lot, thank goodness, now they are very much on board with what we do. I know I learned the reality of the whole thing when I took one up to have it euthanized. They said, "Who's going to pay? It's not free." I responded by saying that it's got to be either the North Carolina Wildlife Resources or National Marine Fisheries. And about five months later I got a phone call from the vet informing me that neither agency would pay. Well, we paid it but we had no budget at all. We had no money—we passed the hat and got the money. I also told them that if there are other turtles we would pay that as well, still not thinking in terms of a hospital. Next thing, a little turtle washes up still very much alive. We get the call, go in my pickup truck that I put my ATV on that I rode the beach all night with, and get one of the volunteers to drive me. We picked this little turtle up, and I learned the first thing I ever knew about taking care of turtles because I patted the turtle and it calmed it down. If it worked for kids, it worked for them too [laughs]. We then took the turtle up to the vet school. That was the turtle that started the whole thing because I thought I was going to leave it up there, I mean it's a hospital, right? They proceeded to tell me that they don't have any place to keep a sea turtle. Well, neither did we. We got back and had to scurry around, and one of our volunteers suggested we put a tank down at the foot of his backyard since he lived on the sound, if we could get our hands on one. We finally got one that Pine Knoll Shores [neighboring town to the north] had thrown on their trash pile. Stuart May [Director of Husbandry and Operations, NC Aquarium] up there at Pine Knolls Shore said that we could have it because he didn't think it would hold up anymore. We still use that tank, by the way. So, the first hospital was one tank in a volunteer's backyard with a 270-foot extension cord, which was actually several extension cords fitted together stretched across his backyard to run the pumps and the water through it. That started the whole thing and from there it just went—as soon as people knew where to take them. Then we decided we should have a place because at that time we had to take turtles down to Florida for a couple of years because we didn't have any place to keep them. Ultimately, we started looking for property and we didn't have any money so the town of Topsail Beach told us they would lease one to us. Once that happened, we were thinking of putting up some sort of prefab thing or something, and try to raise the money. I'm driving home from looking at it and I'm thinking to myself, *How we are going to do this? We don't have any money.* Then all of a sudden, like those things that go across the bottom of the TV, one went across my brain that said *Yes you do—that insurance money.* And our family matched it, and that's how we built that first building. Try to condense that down into four sentences [laughs].

David: That first tank was what year?

Jean: Nineteen ninety-five.

David: Because I called you in 1998 …

Jean: We had just moved into that hospital as of November 7, 1997. It's the eleventh month and the seventh day. Are those lucky numbers or what?

Want to hear something even weirder? When we moved the turtles into this building, without knowing it, it was November 7 [2014]. The hairs stood up, I'm standing up there watching them bring the turtles in saying to myself, *Oh my god! It is November seventh!*

David: I called and I got your name through North Carolina Wildlife Resources. I was starting out and you hadn't been open that long.

Jean: We really didn't intend to open to the public. We finally ended up doing it because people were constantly knocking on the doors and windows wanting to see the turtles [laughs].

David: It's interesting because we were talking about it when we were out there looking at the various tanks of water with the turtles, it defies biological principles but sea turtles respond to humans unlike other reptiles. I believe this. I once witnessed at your old sea turtle hospital that the turtles would pop their heads out of water when they heard you walk near them. I know they have no ears that are visible.

Jean: But they can hear.

David: But they hear, and I know they can't see out of water well so it had to have been your voice that prompted this movement. They were all popping their heads out of each one of the tanks they were in. I thought that was amazing. As I mentioned to you, I was once talking to one of the divers at the New England Aquarium who told me that they had to feed Myrtle first, the wise, old, green sea turtle.

Jean: Yep, she's the diva.

David: Ha, the diva [laughs]. They had to feed her before every other species in the tank because she bothered them relentlessly otherwise. That leads to my question: are sea turtles likely a lot smarter than we give them credit for?

Jean: There is no question about it, and I have evidence, personal evidence. First of all, they play. They show anger. They hone in on anxiousness and they too become anxious. The calmer you can be, the calmer they are going to be. I think most animals are far more sentient than we give them credit for. Yes, they recognize voices. We've had turtles that won't eat from someone whose voice they don't recognize; in fact, most of them won't eat from someone whose voice they don't recognize. They just won't do it. I once had a crusty old guy who was my age—the age I am now but this was twenty years ago—who didn't believe that. This one woman, Emma, fed the turtles everyday by singing to them. She sang [in melodic voice], "Come on over Corey and I'll feed you." She would sing to the turtle while she was feeding it. One day, she wasn't there. Howard went to feed this one particular turtle, Corey, and it wouldn't eat, and he proceeds to tell me that the turtle wouldn't eat. Well, of course, it needs to eat so I told him that you've got to talk to it like Emma does.

"I am not singing to this turtle!" Howard snapped back.

I said, "Howard, if you want the turtle to eat, you're going to have to do it."

Well low and behold after five more frustrating minutes, I hear him singing, "Come on Corey, come on out." And the turtle swam right over and ate. I see it regularly—this thought process. Some people believe very strongly that they're creatures of natural response only, and that they do everything by instinct. They don't really have any thought process. Well, I beg to differ. We had one turtle that was an adult female that weighed about 300 pounds. She'd been there for a while; she was very, very sick. We got to the stage where every morning when we would come in, her tank would be empty of water. The pipe that controls the overflow, that controls the height, would be out. We could not figure out what was happening. I replaced the hardware twice; new pipes, new glue, the whole thing. After a couple of days, we'd come in and there'd she'd be again almost grinning at us, high and dry. One night I was down at the hospital working on paperwork, which is the bane of all of our existences. I would always take a little night-light because the turtles do sleep and the light does bother them. I learned that because I once reached out to pet one as I didn't know it was asleep and I woke it and it freaked us both out. It looked like it was just floating there! Anyhow, so I'm working on my paperwork and I hear this strange noise. I'm there by myself thinking, *What in the heck is that?* It's really weird sounding and it's pitch-black, dark outside. So here I am trying to get the source of the sound, creeping around quietly. I got over to the tank where the noise is coming from, and here is this turtle swimming around her tank. Then she'd stop where the pipe was and she'd grab it in her beak and give it this tug [gestures with mouth]. It wouldn't come, and she'd swim around a few more times with her beak still on the pipe. I stood there watching her, and she finally does it enough times that the pipe comes up and all the water comes out! Now you tell me, is that just instinct that a turtle knows to do that?

David: I'm not sure whether you know the actual number but I wanted to inquire about how many sea turtles you've rehabilitated and released since you opened the hospital in 1997.

Jean: Of course I keep a ballpark figure. We did release turtles prior to 1997 because we did work out in the backyard until we got the building built. I do have a ballpark number: I know it's over 600. That's not counting hatchlings because then it would be in multiples of that. These are all juveniles and up.

David: We were talking earlier about some of the bad habits that we've adopted as sometime careless humans. I've also written and spoke about how the rapid decline of species since the turn of the twenty-first century has been due to what could be called careless behavior on the part of humans. Failing to protect coastal dunes, trolling and long line fishing methods, ocean habitat degradation are some examples. You've witnessed all of these firsthand. How can we create greater awareness of the consequences of our careless behavior?

Jean: First of all, I think we are. We can always do better, and we can always expand our efforts. One of the most rewarding things about having this facility, and having more than 60,000 people a year visiting here, and having an opportunity to pursue one of our missions, which is educating the public about the dangers to sea turtles, are the kids. The kids! Our teachers across the country and around the world are doing a great job teaching kids about the environment, about the planet, about what we are doing wrong, and about how we need to clean up our oceans. Kids come in with the most incredible questions and with the most incredible comments. They know. It's an incredible feeling to look at a group of kids, hear the questions they are asking, and think, *One of them could be the one who finds the key to everything or the one who finds the key to how to get rid of the pacific garbage patch*—which right now we can't do.[2]

I feel that this finds a way to bring this message home to more people because they are into it. For example, little kids coming in with baggies telling me that they had a lemonade stand and saved all their money to help save the sea turtles. We can still do better but...

David: You're right. The next six-year-old could be the inventor of the next TEDs [turtle excluder devices attached to fishing nets].

Jean: That's right.

David: As you know, the book is called *One Green Deed Spawns Another*. All of you have inspired me over the years. I ask the same question because I wanted others to hear from the people who influenced me: if you had one green deed you'd like to see heeded, adopted, and passed on, what would it be and why?

Jean: It would be for everyone to recognize the dangers of the plastics that we have; it's probably our number one. We have become a throw-away society. It sneaked up on us. It certainly did on me. We cannot breathe; we cannot turn in any direction; we cannot go to bed or get up or wash our clothes or eat breakfast or lunch or get in our automobiles or go shopping without constantly running into plastics, plastics, plastics. It is, in my opinion, one of the number one problems we have to deal with. It has invaded our very bodies. We're working at it but other countries are way ahead of the United States outlawing the use of a lot of plastics. I would like to see every country on the planet step up and take a leading role in that. It's very hard, I mean look at this room we're sitting in. Plastic storage cases, for example. We had to really get down to the nitty-gritty with this at the hospital. Over there are K-Cups [Keurig cups]. Guess what that is? Plastic. And throwing them away at this point is too late but you won't see them in here again. [Pointing toward sink] There's a regular coffee pot and a paper filter. It [plastic] is so pervasive and it's becoming more so all the time. You said earlier that there's almost no way that we can stop it. But that can't stop us from trying. We have to have hope and we have to have impetus to try because if we don't try, we are dead. I mean, really dead.

David: I consider it really one of the main culprits behind a lot of the ills of pollution. It is pervasive. You were talking about education earlier; well, you've brought awareness to our coastal environment, and to our waters, in general. You've pushed for more protection for marine species like sea turtles. What's been the biggest positive change since you opened up the hospital?

Jean: I would say awareness—awareness on a number of different levels. First of all, awareness from the point of view of recognizing not just sea turtles but that other creatures out there need our help, a turtle on the side of the road, for example. I get constant comments like "I thought about you today when I stopped to help a turtle and put it going the right way." Got a call this morning about a guy on the beach that said, "I was there when you released a turtle the other day and I just saw a seagull with a broken wing, who do I call?" It's that recognition and awareness that we have created these hazards, and therefore it's our responsibility to help where we can. And then of course the other one is the awareness of our role, every single person's role, in reversing the degradation of our planet. I see hope in that, and I think we need to stress the good things that can happen, and that there can be successes.

David: Right. Many people will tell you that greater awareness has been the biggest change over the last few years. We wouldn't know about these plastic soup patches, like you noted, that are in the Pacific and some of the effects of chemicals in our environment. We know now, we're making some better decisions.

Jean: I want to add something else that I believe in strongly. I have a lot of colleagues who are scientists. I believe in science. I believe in research. But the problems of the world and the ability to have sea turtles in our lives through the coming years and eternity will not be solved [by scientists]. Those questions won't be solved by researchers, by scientists in their laboratories, by even teachers in their classrooms in high schools or universities, any of that. It will be solved by people like any one of us three here and every person we see on the street or in the grocery store, and the little old ladies in tennis shoes, the young kids and the older people. It will take average, ordinary people doing something. If everybody did one thing that they weren't doing. If everyone thought like *OK, my goal is every year I will add one more thing: I won't let the water run when I brush my teeth or I won't forget my reusable bags.* All of us just trying to do one more thing a year, if everybody did that, it would have an incredible impact. Yes, we can save the world. That's the message.

David: That is the essence of the statement "One green deed spawns another." You do one and it will spawn the next one and the next person will take that, and hopefully it will put us on a different direction, a different path. I also wanted to ask about the effect of climate change on sea turtles. I've had people in the book talk about climate change. I ask this because I've often considered sea turtles, certainly females, as environmental guideposts because they spend time on land and in the water. In a relatively short period of time, the blink of an eye for a species that's been around over 50 million years, they've become an endangered species. Will they be able to survive changing ocean conditions, ocean acidification, and changes to the Gulf Stream? What are your thoughts on that?

Jean: Sea turtles survived the cataclysmic events that wiped out the dinosaurs. They're a species that has learned to adapt and to survive whatever was thrown at them. They have a difficult time surviving what we as a species are doing to the planet but they've managed to do even that. At one point, you talked about sand dunes. Well let me tell you this, sea turtles don't see very well on land like you mentioned earlier. They don't always know the difference between a high rise and a sand dune, so they'll actually choose a place on the beach where there's a high rise because to them it looks like a great protective dune. God love 'em, they just don't give up. My favorite expression is *Be like a sea turtle, just keep swimming.* Whatever life throws at you, whatever happens, just keep going. Carl Safina [marine ecologist, writer, and educator] talks about this in *Voyage of the Turtle.* I am paraphrasing but it is something like this: "One thing I've learned from turtles is no matter what happens, no matter if you win or lose, just keep going. That's what important."[3] I think the turtles will find a way; I think they're survivors. I hope so, I've bet my life on it [laughs].

David: I was fortunate to witness, many years ago now, one of your turtle releases. I can't imagine the emotions it must conjure up for you and your volunteers when you set them free after you've saved their lives. I know I was sure moved watching it. Is it a moment of joy or a moment of sadness? Keeping your fingers crossed that you'll never see them again as a patient.

Jean: It's both. It's both joyous and sad. It's frightening because we know the dangers. In order to love the turtles, in order to love anyone, the first step is accepting them for who they are. You can't expect to make them something else, and it's the same with the turtles. The turtles are creatures of the sea, and that's one of the first things that volunteers coming in have to recognize. These turtles are ours for a time, but they are not ours to keep. They're not pets; they're not creatures of a facility. When you care about them, you want to see them be real turtles. A turtle that is free and able to come up and surface and see for miles ahead of them. By the way, I want to tell you a story about when we moved into this building that has nothing to do with your book—I think that there is that fear, and a piece of your heart that goes with them. It is an incredible moment when you see that turtle make the change from dependence on you to *Oh, man, that's home. I smell it. I hear the sound. I feel it in the fiber of my being, and man, I'm out of here.* There is that moment when they push you away and push off to go home—that is the reward. And you know what, for us, that piece of the heart, that hole, then gets filled in by the next turtle that comes in that needs our help. I am frequently questioned about which sea turtle is my favorite of all the turtles we have in here right now. Well my favorite one is usually the one that needs me the most because that's the one I'm focusing on and putting my energy into.

We had a really tough marine who had done a bunch of tours in Afghanistan, et cetera, who came to work for us and just fell in love with one of our turtles. He came out of the water with tears streaming down his face [after the turtle release], and said, "That's what I've worked for." His toughness was softened by his love and appreciation for that animal. And he felt that loss with the release of that animal; he said to me, "I felt what you talked about; I felt that the turtle was telling me it was time to let go."

David: Happy birthday! As you begin your eighth decade on the planet do you ever say *OK, I've done my part, now it's your turn.* You have the right to say that. That's why I wanted to circle back to see you again, and to say that I'm still at it, and you set a wonderful example. In my opinion, this coastal region of the country is far more aware of sea turtles and marine ecology because of you and your volunteers and the work of the hospital. Did you ever imagine that you would have that kind of profound impact?

Jean: Never, but very grateful. And no, I'm not about to rest on my laurels. I will be like Ila Loetscher [1904–2000]. Ila Loetscher was a woman down in Texas, long before sea turtle conservation was a thing. Probably twenty years ago, Ila was close to ninety years old. She's now passed on—look her up, you'll love her—she loved sea turtles and she took in turtles that were injured and maimed, and what have you, and kept them in her swimming pool. Eventually she made her swimming pool a saltwater pool. The cost became too great, so she would make these costumes and put on pageants and plays and let people come in and she'd pass the hat for donations. She would even dress the turtles up in these costumes.[4] One of the most interesting things she did, she noticed one day in her pool that there were Kemp's ridleys mating. She didn't separate species or sexes. I don't know how she got away with that because Kemp's ridleys will attack anything, but she did. In about the period of time the eggs were ready to be deposited, she took that female over to the beach and let her crawl around every day until she actually laid a nest—Kemp's ridleys nest in the daytime. And the nest hatched—a whole series of them. This was an incredible lady. Until the day she died, her volunteers, as her fame in that area grew, would have to carry her out to see her turtles. That's going to be me; I've already told my group here that. That's another reason for the wide doors here; you're going to have to bring me in through the wide doors [laughs]. When somebody has a passion, and you have a passion and I have a passion, you aren't going to give that up easily. That's going to be something that lives in you beyond when you can walk and talk and do those things. Now can I tell you my story about moving in here?

David: Of course.

Jean: One of the things that I loved about the old hospital, and you'll remember this because you were there, was that there was no sound of the running water. When you walked into the building, it was quiet and you could hear the turtles. When they come up, they have to clear the water out before breathing in, and when they open the valve that allows the air to go in, it produces a distinct sound. You can also hear their flippers on the sides of the tank. After all those years in that place, almost twenty, I really wondered if I could go down there at night and hear that sound even when the turtles are gone. Would the walls be a part of that? I don't know for sure but I can't say no. I'm a quirky person [laughs]. But this is what happened here, that day that we talked about, November 7, when they brought the turtles in. We designed sea turtle bay [open area location of the tanks] with high ceilings because I wanted the feeling of openness. I wanted the skylights because I wanted them to have the natural light. It was also a part of our mission to save energy since we don't have to turn lights on in there and use excess energy. So, I thought as I stood there looking at the room, it was dusk and it had been a hard, long day, and I thought, *Oh, I'm so glad that we have these skylights.* Even at dusk the room was beautiful because there was enough light in there to see the tanks. You know that moon you see at dusk while there is still some sun left? I could see that through the skylight as well as the North Star. I wondered if I could hear those sounds because all I heard was water and I now wear hearing aids anyway. I went to the center of the room and I'm listening, listening, listening and all I heard was water. Then I'm like *Wait a minute, yeah I do.* Because I watched the turtles when they came up and when I looked at them, and I don't know if imagined it or if I actually heard it, but I did get that sound a little bit. Then the next thing in my mind was *What are they doing?* Every turtle was coming up clearing, breathing, and looking up, looking at the sky. I hadn't thought about that part of it. Some of those turtles were seeing the sky for the first time in more than a year with their injuries. And they've done it ever since. It still makes me cry.

CHAPTER 6

*"As we say, sustainable isn't just environmental.
It has to be economic."*

Photo by Alex Mahood

Thomas Herlihy

Organic Waste Engineer

Farmer

Worm Power

The Herlihys are one of the significant families that spanned most of my life in Geneseo, New York, my hometown, and the many years since I left. The senior Herlihys, John and Myra, relocated the family there in the early 1970s, where the patriarch, John, joined the State University College at Geneseo (now SUNY Geneseo) faculty in 1973 working in the same department as Dad. Tom, the youngest of three boys, was one grade behind me in high school. Geneseo was, and is, a picturesque college town nestled in the fertile Genesee Valley. Tom claimed not only the same bucolic hometown but many of the same teachers and friends. But few could have predicted the course of our lives back then, and nobody for certain would have brought up worms.

In 2002, Tom moved his family from Pennsylvania to Greensboro, North Carolina, where I was living, and we had the opportunity to rekindle our friendship. Tom was working as an environmental engineer in Greensboro when he shared his concept for the vermicomposting business with me. Back then, the idea of organic waste management powered by worms was such an original concept. and still is to this day.

By 2005, Tom and his wife and daughters had moved back to his hometown of Geneseo. Ultimately, his vermicompost operation, Worm Power, broke ground in Avon, New York, just north of Geneseo. Once, while on a family vacation, I took my young boys for a visit. We still laugh today at the photos we took of Tom on the farm and the boys fighting over which one of them was going to get to sit on the tractor or "mobile" as Christopher called it back then.

Interview—2014

Tom and I got together in Las Vegas in May because at my request he had agreed to speak at our third NEWH Green Voice program at the Hospitality Design Expo in Las Vegas. The hospitality industry is a massive consumer of the world's resources and an industry responsible for a prodigious amount of waste. Vermicompost could serve the industry well, including Las Vegas, in several key ways: by enriching soil and improving water retention, by cutting

CO_2 emissions from food and municipal waste disposal, and by reducing chemical dependency overall. I knew the story of Worm Power would be intriguing to many in the industry but especially to my sustainability cohorts. To see Tom stand toe to toe with top-level sustainable executives from the hospitality community in Las Vegas was wholly satisfying to me. Tom's organic waste management expertise added a truly unique element to the discourse. One of the participants, the Executive Chef from Mandalay Bay, Susan Wolfla, who holds a BS in Cell and Development Biology from Purdue, told me before the event, "I'm really looking forward to meeting the worm farmer." And despite her hectic schedule, Susan got that chance, as did Dina Belon (chapter 9) who conducted a Green Voice interview with Tom.

I emailed Tom about *One Green Deed* a couple months before the Christmas holiday to see if he'd be interested in participating. I knew I wanted to dedicate a chapter to Tom's vision, and I suggested that we take advantage of the holiday to get together and record the interview. I kind of forgot that holidays also mean *holidaze* but Tom and I boldly agreed to an interview on the twenty-sixth of December. I invited my oldest son, Alex, and my stepdaughter, Samantha, as well as my trusty audio expert and wife, Maryann, to join me. The twenty-sixth of December turned out to be a quiet Friday for the now largest vermicomposting farm in the world so Tom was able to spend extra time with us at Worm Power headquarters. He gave us a thorough tour of the farm, explaining the science and agriculture behind Worm Power. The large digester beds, home to millions of worms in the process of decomposing dairy poop, are odorless, and filled with a soil material as smooth and pristine as you'll ever touch. Tom's capacity to explain the story of worm composting and the importance of organic, fertile soil, is not something to be missed. His worms create the organic fertilizer that benefits professional growers from vineyards, golf courses, and orchards across the United States and beyond. Many regional vineyards and breweries have become Worm Power's best friends. Consumers like us are constantly searching for more and more sustainable food and beverages all the time. Tom's products are making that happen all over the globe.

Tom's compelling story is also unique because it has geographically taken him full circle—back to his roots, back to where he grew up. Sharing Tom's journey and success is particularly satisfying to me.

David: First things first, today is December 26, 2014. If this doesn't go perfectly then we'll blame it on the season's merriment or the sugarplums.

Tom: I've been deposed a couple of times so I can do this.

David: The very hardworking and love-making earthworms out there, those hermaphrodites, are what species? I know they are a type of red worm.

Tom: Right, people often just call them red worms. If you're asking me, now putting on my science hat, they're in the epigeic family. They're in the surface-dwelling family of worms, I guess there are probably two or three hundred species. I probably have four or five different species here. So, I've seen the fetida [*Eisenia fetida*], I've seen the andrei [*Eisenia andrei*], the Perionyx [*Perionyx excavatus*], but they have to be in the epigeic family, the kind that live in the surface layer—as opposed to the kind that have permanent burrows like in your soil, which are in the anecic family, and are invasive. There are basically no native North American earthworms until you get to about South Carolina—they are all post pilgrims up here.

David: Tell me a little bit about how you got interested in starting Worm Power, what your background was. The whole story is fascinating—not many people have taken the path that you've taken.

Tom: Sure, I certainly never ever thought that I would be running a worm farm at fifty-one years of age. I was a geek geek so my undergraduate was physics and math but I worked summers living here in the Genesee Valley on a dairy farm. I always thought was a pretty nice juxtaposition, spending nine months of the year living totally inside my head and the other three months I was a human forklift. When I graduated college, be it my moral upbringing or whatever, I joined the Peace Corps. I thought that if I was going to be practicing some of these more progressive liberal philosophies I should at one point in my life have actually practiced what I preach. And I did tell them I didn't want to teach because I came from a whole family of teachers and everything so I really didn't want to be a teacher. Having worked on a dairy farm obviously equipped me to be an International Agricultural Extension Agent [laughs]. The Peace Corps is very good at that sort of thing. So, I worked on an AID [USAID] project—seed multiplication, growing millet in West Africa in a country called Niger, North of Nigeria, South of Libya, and Algiers. I really enjoyed that experience. I actually thought I wanted to work overseas in agriculture the rest of my life but a degree in physics does not exactly make one marketable in the agricultural world. Later, in graduate school I looked at something that could combine the background I had with the direction I wanted to move into. I went to Penn State and received a master's in Agriculture and Biological Engineering, where they accepted most of my physics stuff, and it positioned me much better. I met my wife in graduate school but she didn't want to go live in West Africa so I had to find work here in the states, which led me to become an environmental engineer, a position where I could use basic engineering principles with biological systems to do remediations. I did a lot of work cleaning up after the coal industry—revegetating coal mine sites, cleaning up acid mine drainage sites. Also, using biological husbandry in wastewater treatment plants, and being able to handle human manures and human wastes better. Ultimately, I had about a fifteen- or sixteen-year career, whatever it was, almost twenty years, climbing the ladder in the corporate engineering world, always very much enjoying the creative, problem-solving aspect but not so much the corporate structure and actually managing people, to be honest. By the time I left, I was running the North Carolina office for an engineering firm, and half my day was people coming in and closing the door behind them. People never close the door behind them when it's good, right? They're going to complain and I'm not the most empathetic, I'm an engineer.

I had done a lot of composting and using biological systems to fix basically human-made woes and to blunt the worst part of it. We can't be nonimpacting but we can be minimally impacting. I had a project in Australia, of all places, and it was their version of the thruway and the toilet was a vermicomposting toilet because they had no water. A rest area in the middle of nowhere, and I'm reading the thing and saw where it was. I decided to extend my stay and I saw, what was at the time, probably the largest vermicomposting facility in the world. So, I went and saw them and thought they had something, but these guys didn't have a clear idea what they were doing. Boy, I hope they never read this—nice guys but they didn't understand engineering and marketing.

Large-scale vermicomposting requires you to understand animal husbandry, the raising of the worms—there's the engineering of how you run a large-scale animal agricultural operation, and the other thing is you have to make a product that is used in plant production. You have to know engineering, you have to know animal husbandry, and you have to know plant agriculture. If you don't know those things, then you're just doing the "*Field of Dreams* mentality," I call it—if I build it, they will come. And there has not been a large history of success in our industry with that. We've had a lot of spectacular train wrecks in the vermicomposting industry. People have gone through millions of dollars with nothing to show for it in the end really.

David: What year was that? Do you remember?

Tom: It was 2001 when I went to Australia. When I came back, I talked to my engineering firm and I said we ought to bring this technology to the U.S. We could bring it to some nice progressive municipalities. Find the right people that want to do this, and we could become the national leader and carve out our technology niche. Instead, they were going, "Where are the engineering fees? Where are the billable hours? Billable hours, billable hours, billable hours—what part of our business model don't you understand?" [laughs] That sort of thing. But I did understand it. I'd been working in that space, I had to land multimillion-dollar projects on time and on budget, working with the regulators, working with the clients, and working with the public. The engineering aspect was probably down to 15 to 20% of my job by the end. It was really project management; learning to put strange groups to work together, and then also making sure to deliver on your promise, so to speak. Anyhow, how we started the company was really at the craps table in Vegas [laughs]. I had an angel investor who came to hear me give a talk at the U.S. Composting Council, which happened to be in Vegas. He had a very good night, and he asked what it would take for me to really build a facility like that [vermicomposting facility]. Well to start, I would have to leave my job, which was a pretty good job, and it would probably take me six months to do a true feasibility study, and find out where in the nation we could build it. Which waste segment we were going to tackle: human manure, dairy manure, chicken manure, swine manure, food waste, yard waste? Then find a facility, a place, find someone who could let us colocate and then really build the business model. What is it going to cost us to build it? What's it going to cost us to operate it? Can we really operate it? Then, if we have our material, can we really sell it? We had five major obstacles when we started it. But he bankrolled it, and at the end of six months I identified a dairy here in the Genesee Valley. I was living in North Carolina. Even though I'm from here, literally, it is strange that the engineering took me back here to the Genesee Valley. This is one of the great dairy concentrations on the planet. You have 120,000 cows in a ninety-mile radius around you right now. Again, this is a cow, which outweighs us 10:1. This isn't like sheep in New Zealand where there are more sheep than people, we're talking about a cow, which out-biomasses us 10:1 or 1,800 pounds to 180 pounds. Well, so you know the numbers came out, I really thought we could do it but then we had to go raise some more money. That was one bit of money, and the next bit of money was to build what we thought was kind of the pilot facility, which was going to be the largest in the country but from an engineering point of view, it was nothing but a pilot. It was never intended to be profitable; it was to prove that I could integrate it into animal agriculture, a real working dairy farm. The dairies are not out to prove anything with vermicomposting, you know, they have their own issues with manure management. And that we can build it for what we thought we could build it for. Then from a biology point of view, that I could raise millions of earthworms in a real production system. That our operating budget to keep those worms happy was reasonable and it could work in our business model and then again, that we had an end product that I could sell for about ten times what compost sells for to offset all these other costs. It took about five, six years, but we kind of went *check, check, check* down the list, and we were all set to go great big guns, and that would have been 2008. If you don't remember what happened in 2008, the great recession just about finished me. I had global agribusinesses courting us. Then it went from they weren't courting me, to not answering my phone calls, to outright telling me, "Don't call us, we'll call you." In the course of about six months it was very, very scary. We were circling the drain, but we had a dedicated staff. I had two colleagues, and myself, work for no money for nine months to keep the facility running while we were waiting for things to turn—so that's dedication. I will always remember those two guys and one of them is still sitting out there right now. The other person still works for us part-time. Well, we got through that. The pilot facility was sold out by February of every year—sales committed. We'd produce a quarter million pounds a year, but it wasn't making the company enough money because it was a pilot facility. So then in 2010 I was able to raise another huge chunk of money, and we were able to do an eightfold expansion in our production. But by 2012, I had a parting of the ways with that party. They weren't bad people; I just felt they didn't understand what they had gotten into. I probably knew that at the time but I was desperate for the funding. We had to survive. We got new investors and we feel that most of our work now is driving adoption. We really don't have anything left to prove. I can make vermicompost from just about any organic waste. We have a very valid business model. The last thing for me to do is to drive adoption into production horticulture. I feel we have 100 dairies that would sign up, that would want us to locate on their dairy. Now the issue is with the growers; it's driving adoption with the commercial growers. That's also a two- to three-year process to get a customer because this is their livelihood. They want to do the right things but they're not going to endanger the paycheck. "What do I got? I have this forty-acre strawberry patch. This is what I'm leaving my kids and I have to put food on the table."

David: That's a lot of risk.

Tom: Uh, that was a long answer to a simple question.

David: And here you are today.

Tom: And here I am today.

David: With the largest vermicomposting facility on the planet. That's quite a story.

Tom: Yeah, we like to think we're a nice blend of technology. That's why I wanted to go into biological engineering. About 80% of what we do here is science but there's still 20% of what we do that is craft like wine making or leather making, you know. If you don't understand the basic science, you can't be good at it, but to be great at it requires tweaking and understanding the little things that you have to keep adjusting on the fly.

David: What's interesting is you've done some creative things also to contain some of those costs—your use of rainwater, some of the ways that you're able to minimize energy use. That's also obviously a testament to your engineering skills.

Tom: And we do, we try to be as minimally impacting as we can. Again, minimally impacting. We try to use appropriate technology wherever but also realizing that American ag [agriculture] is built on the precept that you'll spend ten dollars in capital to avoid one dollar in labor. It just is! A capital item can be depreciated over time and labor goes up. Again, it's difficult to attract labor as we do work with manure. It's a shitty job [laughter]. It's difficult at times. This is western New York where it can be 100 [degrees] in August and ten below in January. We have a 100-degree swing in six months, and we are outside in it for a third of the day. It's not like scooting from the mall to your car, you know, you're in it. It's hard to get people to sign up.

David: I'm reading this book right now, *Living Downstream*, about the causal relationship between synthetic chemicals and carcinogens.[1] I didn't truly grasp the importance of organic soil. The author is making the point that some of the synthetic chemicals that are used as pesticides or herbicides may have a link to cancers. She is a cancer survivor from a very agriculturally intense region of the U.S. Your soil is critical potentially not only for the health of the soil but for health of people.

Tom: There's a great book you should read I think it's called *Dirt: The Erosion of Civilization*.[2] Most of the major civilizations that have collapsed in the world are because they didn't treat their soil well. It's a great book and links anthropology to soil science, which you normally wouldn't think of as two disciplines being related. So we look at agriculture—there's always physical, chemical, and biological properties. We always talk about the three legs of the tripod that all fertility is based on, so productive soils have great physical properties, chemical properties, and biological properties. The first agriculture revolution was the domestication of animals and tillage. We've learned how to modify the physical properties of soil. There was a great big bloom in production. Instead of going around and picking wild berries, you could actually start to cultivate some crops, and human civilization takes another quantum step up the ladder. Well, post–World War II we had the bomb factories left over. We learned how to synthesize nitrogen from the atmosphere so there's a great fertilizer boom. We learned how to modify the chemical properties of the soil. That's the green revolution of the 1950s. It's interesting to note that fertilizers have not been around that long, or agrochemicals, in general. This is a post-WW II phenomenon. It was a huge boost in productivity. Then you could even start manipulating soils that probably would never have been productive but just by the addition of chemicals you could make them productive. You could bring in water via aqueducts, and we could farm large regions of the country that were never farmable before. But what's the third leg that's remaining? What's this last great revolution? It's going to be biologically based. The 10,000 microbial species in a gram of soil, which is the size of your thumbnail, the approximate 10,000 species of soil bacteria, fungi, and actinomycetes [a heterogeneous collection of bacteria that form branching filaments], of which we only know about 2% through PCR [polymerase chain reaction], the DNA. Of that 2% we've identified the functionality of about 2% of that. You can say we're at about a .04% of full understanding. That's really where Worm Power fits in. Regulators say we're a fertilizer, but you don't really buy us for the chemicals. We are really like yogurt for the soil. Look at the Great Plains, for example, it hosted one of the great animal concentrations on the planet: the bison. They eat a lot of forage, right? They're cows. No one ever fertilized the Great Plains. It was because they had these natural functioning ecosystems. The soil microbial communities act to convert the parent material [soil] to the nutrients for the plant. You get the whole natural nutrient cycling going on. What the agrichemicals have done is basically take out the need to have the natural nutrient cycling done. Instead, we have put ourselves in the place of feeding the plants. But then you're also disrupting that soil ecology by the use of these harsher agrichemicals. Consequently, you've turned the plants from a self-reliant system into one that is basically addicted to chemicals and to our full-time care.

We think about 10% of our customers are certified organic. Most of them we call "hybrid organic" because if they're going to lose a crop, they are going to spray against a pest. Again, if you're a vineyard you're not going to lose your entire crop. "Bad year to be me, I'm going to lose every grape." These growers know the soil is what they are leaving their kids. This land is where they live and they work, and they take a great deal of pride in what they do. They're all wanting to use more sustainable systems and sustainable approaches, but you just have to make it palatable for them. Reduce the risk, explain to them why it works, and show them that by adopting this they can maintain a similar level of production. It doesn't have to be better than chemicals, just ensure a similar level of productivity. One of the fallacies in organic is to say that you can get more production than from chemicals. Don't lie, if you don't know. It's credibility, again. We don't need to make wacky claims. All we really need to say is that if you switch to these kinds of materials, you can maintain your same economic return on your land, and you're going to be conserving your land better to leave to somebody else. To me, that's where we need to head with these things. That's because that's sustainable. As we say, sustainable isn't just environmental. It has to be economic. If people can't make a living, it's not sustainable.

David: Yeah, people, profit, planet.

Tom: It doesn't have to be rapacious profit though.

David: That actually could be your answer if you wanted. If there were one green deed you would like to see heeded, implemented, passed on, what would it be and why?

Tom: What the concept of being sustainable really is to me is that there's no such thing as being nonimpacting. I guess the deed is to come to the realization that to have a civilization the way we have it, we have to start thinking in time scales that we don't think of as people. It's not just the profits for the next quarter—being sustainable means that you need to leave land and water resources for the next generation so they can husband it and steward it to get a living off of it as well. Somebody has to be a primary producer because we all just can't make margins on each other's transactions. That's a different one. Stay away from that one for now. I'll get in trouble with my investors!

David: But you're providing in a very big way the sustainable solutions you're talking about.

Tom: Again, to be sustainable doesn't mean we all have to live on a half-acre farm on a hillside in Vermont. I'm not saying we all have to become organic farmers and grow all of our own food in our backyard. But either through supporting producers that can produce things in a sustainable way, modifying our consumption habits and modifying our financial appetites, we can really work at having a more sustainable society. I mean especially,

I'm not America, love it or leave it, but we are very uniquely positioned to be a sustainable society. We just have an incredible abundance of resources; we don't have to undergo hardships, if we undertake this sooner rather than later. A crash course is more expensive and more disruptive to the social contract. I really think for minimal involvement right now. . . if food costs you a nickel more for a loaf of bread or a gallon of milk, I don't really think that disrupts the social contract too much. It wouldn't even need to be for the long term, just during this transition. The transition's going to be the hard part. Change is hard. Amen, I can swear to that one.

David: We don't want to be in a situation where we're so devoid of resources like some of the European nations that have had to completely convert because we do have an abundance here in America; we're land rich, resource rich, and water rich in this region. I mean, sustainability should not be out of the realm of possibility for us.

Tom: Well, I don't know if that's your green deed: the thought of what *sustainable* means, and to think about it a little bit.

David: Yeah, and teach that. Educate. Your tour that you give is your means of teaching. You're obviously from a family of teachers like I am, and our fathers taught together in the same department. Every time you take somebody through here you're doing that [teaching].

Tom: Right.

David: That's kind of interesting, because I'd like to think that part of my influence was my parents. Certainly, the way they raised us. I mean, we weren't starving but they were very careful about the use of resources and taught us those lessons. I always make the joke of Dad putting solar panels on the house in the 1970s, which was pretty forward thinking— gambling on those few days of sunshine here in this region.

Tom: Especially the 1970s technology solar panels.

David: Yeah, I think there are sixteen days of sun or something like that here in Geneseo [laughs].

Tom: Yeah, right.

David: Was there somebody who influenced you? Inspired you?

Tom: From working on a dairy farm, Floyd Anderson or Mo. If I called him Floyd, he'd go, "Who?" So, yes, from working at Mo Anderson's dairy farm in York, New York. I had led a very cerebral life. We had a very academic family; we discussed Louis the Sixteenth at the dinner table. And then I would go to work at a dairy farm, it was just an entirely different world to me. I enjoyed getting dirt under my fingernails. Then seeing that I could merge into—you wouldn't call him an environmentalist by any stretch or form but he had that connection to the land—what you have to take care of sort of thing. That was eye opening to me. One of the people who helped me with a major loan for this expansion is Doug Tompkins, founder of the North Face and Esprit clothing lines. An ardent environmentalist, I guess, would be an expression to use for him. Even with the corporate culture back then—he and Yvon Chouinard from Black Diamond and Patagonia. Black Diamond was about climbing, they were climbers. He's a Catskills guy, the Gunks [Shawagunks climbing area near New Paltz, New York], ice climbing, you know. But anyhow, that whole idea that you can have a successful company that doesn't have to be based on the rapacious business model. This concept was exemplified in Yvon's book, *Let My People Go Surfing*.[3] If the surf was nice, they closed the company and let everyone go surfing and return to work after. So many companies say they value their employees, but they just say it.

Doug Thompkins is a great aesthete. You can just tell. He likes to photograph beautiful agro-ecosystems as works of art on their own. And they are. He flies his small plane in Argentina, photographing some beautiful landscapes and farms. He feels that preservation doesn't have to mean that no one gets to touch anything. You can have functioning agro-ecosystems that have multiple functional values and still make food, but it doesn't have to look like or behave like a monoculture cornfield.

David: That's part of the issue that I take with farming. They're not small farms anymore. They're big agro-businesses; they're fully supporting mono-crop farming practices.

Tom: It's easier.

David: It's easier but it also tends to be chemically intensive.

Tom: Yes, it is, but I always try to understand both sides of the table. Some industries in the agro-business world can be brutal, especially in pursuit of yields. The dairy industry is unique because it's still mainly family farms around here. It doesn't lend itself readily to that business model. On the other hand, we believe we can show production agriculture a different way.

One of the hardest points in organic agriculture is weed management, because we don't want to spray herbicides. Weeds do compete for water and nutrients against the plants you're trying to grow. The reason Roundup exists is you can't have hundreds of people with hoes digging up every weed across the corn belt.

David: I was hoping we wouldn't bring up the *R* word.

Tom: We're finding out now that they can build different agricultural implements and practices that can do some of that weeding at tractor scale. We are also learning that some cover crops can make living mulch mats to keep weeds down. You time these cover crops so its water and nutrient needs don't coincide with the crop cycle you're trying to grow. Basically you knock them down and create a living mulch layer around your plants. It's dead and it's down but weeds can't germinate through it, thus all the water and nutrients go to the plant you're trying to nurture. Learning agro-ecosystems is basically biological engineering. We can work our way around many issues but in the meantime, you can't convert the entire state of Kansas from corn right now. I don't know enough to know that I guess, but we do know other ways. You shouldn't cast a stone until you walk a mile in their shoes at times. But I believe we can show a different way to grow crops.

David: You figure that here were these poor Vietnam vets getting exposed to Agent Orange and coming back and getting cancer. Knowing full well what caused it—so let's take Agent Orange and start putting it on our crops.

Tom: Actually, it was the other way around. They knew what Agent Orange was—and basically, it's a[n] up-plant growth regulator. Believe it or not, it doesn't kill the plant; it makes the plant grow itself to death. It overly stimulates the plants to grow. They grow so fast that they basically grow themselves to death. What's amazing is that these chemicals are active in the parts per billion. They are basically hormones, they're called plant growth hormones, PG. But it's ounces to the acre, that's nothing. So again, it's probably not like the chemist that sat there and thought, *What the hell could I do wrong, I'm putting down three ounces to the acre. How bad could this stuff be?*

David: No, it's interesting. Since we're talking about World War II, a lot of these materials that were being developed were basically, some were, anyhow, being developed for the war effort. Then postwar, all these chemicals had to be used for something, and these chemical companies decided on this application.

Tom: We've built the infrastructure of these multimillion-dollar chemical factories. What the hell you going to do with them now? Again, so you're the person in charge of the chemical factory and you have a fiscal responsibility to your shareholders and they're all going [knocks on table], "Department of Defense, we are not going to be buying any more TNT. What are we going to do with this factory now?" Don't lay off a thousand workers who have families that they're trying to feed. So the guy is sitting there thinking, *Well, that's nitrogen. I know who needs nitrogen. Damn farms, that's who needs nitrogen.* There wasn't a Montgomery Burns from the Simpsons [television series] saying, "Excellent, now I have them in my power" [in accent]. It was likely just some guy thinking I got this factory that makes nitrogen.

David: I know.

Tom: I know you know. Again, my thing is never try to demonize the other side because most of the time they are good people. I really believe most people are good. In their heart of hearts, they would make the right decision. Again, I think about those things; they didn't set out to turn the world into chemical agriculture just trying to make some money.

David: I know, they aren't nefarious people trying to rule the world but …

Tom: Now there a couple of people out there but the vast majority of them aren't. An example I use all the time is Kodak here [Rochester, New York]. These guys invented the digital camera that killed them. I think at one time the largest concentration of chemical engineers on the planet was in Rochester, New York. This company also had billions of dollars in chemical engineering infrastructure, and they were the largest silver buyer in the world. I'm guessing these guys knew in their heart of hearts, the digital revolution was coming. They didn't know the speed, but they had to be thinking, *What am I going to do with these massive chemical factories? I have a gigantic chemical factory, what am I going to do with it? How will it transition into the digital age?* Seriously, everybody went from having a camera and then in five years nobody had a film camera. We all used to sing "Don't take my Kodachrome away" and say it's a "Kodak moment" [popular slogan developed by Eastman Kodak].[4] It was in the American lexicon. Everybody had a family photo album, and now it's just gone. What I guess I'm trying to say is maybe we can do the same thing with chemical agriculture, I don't know.

David: Last question, coming back to your hometown, starting this business, doing good as you are, is a great story. I'm very proud of you, and I'm sure a lot of people around here are also, so I hope you take pride in what you're doing because you're doing a great thing for the community, for this whole region. You're impacting farmers around the world. We're eating healthier food because of you, Tom, so I hope you take great pride in that.

Tom: I do; it's been a struggle of near biblical proportions to me professionally and personally. Then again some mornings when I'm shaving, looking at myself in the mirror, I reflect on the fact that this is my life's work. I used to shy away from using that expression but this is my professional life's work. This is it. We don't think we're bomb-throwing radicals; we like to say we're the tugboats. American production agriculture is a supertanker. We don't want to be the pirates trying to take it over, we want to be the little tugboat in the front to just kind of push it in a new direction. And next thing you know, the whole supertanker and the whole fleet will start veering off to the left. Not to the right, to the left [laughs]. It is, and we're one of many tugboats out there. The movement is about credibility; it's all about credibility. You've probably heard me saying that I have what I believe but I also know what I can say. And I always try, but at times I have to leave bullets in the gun because if I use one too many then I could collapse nine or ten years of effort.

David: Well, knowing you as long as I have, I have faith in you.

Tom: The financial model I think is more broken than the agricultural model but that's a whole other discussion.

CHAPTER 7

"There have been people trying to save the forest who have addressed the home furnishings industry for decades."

Photo by Margaret Krome-Lukens, From the Mountain

Susan Inglis

From the Mountain

Sustainable Furnishings Council

I realize that I'm drawn to persons who have an innate sense of goodness, especially when it comes to protecting the environment. In 2006 I met another of those persons, a woman named Susan Inglis, who had volunteered to help a fledgling movement steer the residential furniture industry toward sustainability. She had been at the genesis of the movement that was founded by Gerry Cooklin, an early proponent of certified wood labeling and sustainability in general, who started a company called South Cone in 1994. Although the commercial furniture market had been advancing sustainable wood certifications for years, the residential furniture makers, for the most part, had lagged far behind. Gerry had worked continuously to sustain resources in South America from whence he hailed, and Susan had been doing the same thing for international textiles. I offered my help to the new organization since I had prior involvement in the commercial furnishings market as a green manufacturer. The combination of volunteers coalesced into an organization called the Sustainable Furnishings Council, which I continue to support to this day. Susan was one of the dozen original volunteers and from that first organizational meeting, we developed a lasting friendship. It was no surprise to me that she vaulted to a role of leadership within the organization. Every organization needs a person like Susan Inglis, and the Sustainable Furnishings Council was fortunate to get the authentic one. From the committees I joined and from the chair positions I held within the organization, I witnessed what one person could do to create consensus. SFC had a perpetual feeling of energy and accomplishment because of the efforts of Susan and Gerry. At that time, she shared with me stories of her travels to the remote areas of the world and her interest in supporting diverse cultures. In a time when women are oppressed in so many regions of the globe, Susan could be called courageous. To put what I mean in perspective, I was a robust twenty-year-old college student in 1983 when I got mugged in Morocco, and Susan had been there years before.

As I transitioned off the SFC board and began to focus on the hospitality furnishings market, I had fewer opportunities to work with Susan. Although we would exchange ideas and continue to network, it wasn't until 2007 that Susan approached me about an opportunity to consult to an organization called SENADA. Funded by USAID (United States Agency for International

Development), SENADA was a four-year Indonesian competitive development project created by DAI, Development Alternatives Incorporated. Susan had suggested my name as a trainer for the SENADA program, which was headquartered in Jakarta, and Jogjakarta, on the Indonesian island of Java. She had already completed her work on the project by the time I left for Indonesia in late 2007. My role was to train home accessories or handicraft manufacturers on the principles of sustainability in an effort to make their products more valuable and competitive in the global market. Despite my initial fear about going to a country of a dominant religion I barely understood and a place still considered moderately safe because of terrorism, I had one of the best experiences of my life. And Susan beat me there as well.

I had sought out Susan to join me in a number of sustainability talks for NEWH during my role as Vice President of Sustainable Hospitality for the organization. She had to back out in 2009 but in 2012, Susan participated in the premier Green Voice Conversations at HD Expo in Las Vegas, which included Katie Fernholz (chapter 4). I had connected Susan and Katie a few years earlier, which resulted in Katie's membership and board position on the Sustainable Furnishings Council. Both Susan and Katie were eloquent and informative and the NEWH Green Voice Conversations began on a promising note.

Interview—2015

I borrowed son Christopher's car to make the hour-long drive to Chapel Hill from Greensboro, North Carolina, to meet up with Susan. We met on a picture-perfect summer day. There is truth to the description, Carolina blue. I'd been in steady contact with Susan for most of 2015 due to our mutual interest in natural materials and sustainable products. We've been pitching the same premise that products can be made more ecologically for years. In fact, we'd been brainstorming about Barbara Filippone's coco fiber and latex foam (chapter 12), for some time. Long before the HBO documentary, *Toxic Hot Seat*, both of us were well aware of the toxicity of fire retardants in our upholstered furniture.[1] Susan operates much of her business, From the Mountain, out of her home, and was in the midst of inspecting a new order of fiber when I arrived. She and I sat down at her dining table and I soon found out that Susan is very capable of multitasking: the phone rang, her associate, Margaret, burst through the front door among other interruptions. Truth be told, I was partly distracted by the activity on the back porch stemming from her incredible butterfly bush. It's way too easy to just say Susan has southern charm; it's way too easy to tag her as a tree hugger, and I imagine she's perfectly comfortable with that. But in my near ten years of knowing Susan Inglis, I've seen what one caring person can do and none of it has been easy. Her passion is genuine, and for many of us, that is the litmus test for environmentalists. Susan has inspired me to believe that we anthropologists and we Spanish majors can enact real change.

David: You got your anthropology degree from University of North Carolina at Chapel Hill. That prompted you to take interest in other cultures and want to travel as much as you have. Name some of the places you've traveled in your lifetime because I know you've been to a lot of remote places.

Susan: Yeah, I have. Really it's because of my love of travel and the love of travel I inherited that I ended up with an anthropology degree. When I started college, I thought I would study art history. I kept quitting to do more interesting things than be in school, and it usually involved travel. The last semester of my high school I spent in Greece, and I had such a good time that I decided to stay there for the summer instead of coming back to graduate. I did ultimately come back in time to go to college at UNC. So, one of the times when I quit I went back to Greece, and another time when I quit I worked in England for about a year because my father was British and I have lots of family there. I was with my then-boyfriend, and we lived in Southern France for a while, and then we went to Morocco. And when I say "lived" I mean live like young people do, a few months at a time is living there [laughs]. I'd been to many places. My parents made sure that we knew a little bit about the wider world. For me, personally, the first time we went to England to visit my father's family, when I was eleven, was when I learned the world was bigger than Chowan County, North Carolina, and that was good news. I was really, really glad to know there was more possibility.

I think it was those things that led me to studying what I studied that led up to an anthropology degree. I didn't go to school to study anthropology but somehow I landed on an anthropology degree. I have used that information in what I've done in my career. My career has been a winding path like most interesting ones are probably [laughs]. I have always made use of what I learned in studying cultural anthropology. I have been to lots of countries before I started working as well as since I've been working.

David: Being in a remote village in the Himalayas is certainly a far cry from Chapel Hill, North Carolina.

Susan: It is. Nepal is one of the places I've traveled, and my work in Nepal has been in eastern Nepal in the Makalu-Barun Conservation Area.

David: And that is your inspiration behind your business, From the Mountain? How did From the Mountain get started?

Susan: That's right. From the Mountain is a small business that started out of my whole life orientation. I grew up in a family that makes a lot of things with our hands as a hobby, so when the time came for me to make a living I didn't have enough sense to get a job, so I wondered, *Hmm, what could I make?* I had two little children and I was bound and determined to be an at-home mom with them. Initially I started a custom sweater business, and I did everything with my own two hands. Eventually, I was doing production through an economic development program in West Virginia providing self-employment opportunities to women in their homes there. Through that organization in West Virginia, I had the great opportunity to go to Nepal to work with an interesting exotic fiber. The organization called The Mountain Institute had a project in eastern Nepal on the edge of a conservation area. They wanted to generate income for villages, and they wanted to do it using traditional materials and skills. The basic idea was to support life as it was there and to give villagers a way of making a living as an alternative to going into the parks and poaching the wildlife. I ended up flying to a remote airport and I walked for three days before finally getting to those artisans. The fiber they worked with is called "nettle cloth." It comes from the inner bark of the giant stinging nettle plant. It's sort of . . . well . . . like a rough linen, and it's a traditional fiber there, possibly the oldest known fiber to be processed. Well before people were processing cotton or silk, for instance. It's actually a weedy plant that grows only in the middle altitudes of the Himalayas. My job ostensibly was to get the products of these weavers, spinners, and knitters, to the U.S. market. It was clear to me that nobody was going to happen along and buy the stuff even if I had developed the perfect product there, so I decided I would have to begin importing it, which is what I did. My sweater business was transitioning to a home textile business anyway so I ended up adding on these tabletop items that were made of nettle cloth. Because it had similar characteristics to linen, it was very good for place mats. So just in the moment I decided I'm going to give this a go. I ordered a load of them, which arrived six months later, long after I'd been back to the U.S., and took them around to various shops and met with pretty good reception overall. And that is really when From the Mountain was born. The name From the Mountain occurred to me in a dream when I was there in the Himalayas. The two trips I made to Nepal, by the way, were in 1993 and 1994. I had only been working with the women in Nepal, but after my second trip, the men approached me about their products that included baskets, so soon after, I began importing baskets also. And my business continued in that manner as an import business selling into the home furnishings industry until the war got too bad in Nepal and it was impossible to work there anymore with the Maoist uprising, and the civil war. And unfortunately, the work petered out. I haven't been there in many, many years but I'm pleased to report that others are working with the fiber in that region now and I do see their products on the market every now and then. In the meantime, From the Mountain evolved into a brokering business working not just in Nepal but after that in Guatemala and Kyrgyzstan, for example, and then in many countries in Latin America. There were various artisan enterprises that I could draw on to get products to the home furnishings market, which was where most of my focus was back then. I met these small, mostly women-owned businesses through consulting projects on publicly funded programs that hired me to get artisan skills to new markets. I've been hired to do product development or to develop entrepreneurial skills or simply to make market connections. It naturally evolved into a brokering business, so I can continue to draw on the skills and products of these artisans. It was one of those projects just a few years ago that brought me in contact with Afghan cashmere producers. They had only a few weeks left on the project, and just one tradeshow left so they asked me to help make some introductions for them. Well, we did, and a big fashion company, J.CREW, bought yarn, and I knew it wasn't going to be successful unless I handheld it so I took on being broker for these cashmere producers when the project ended. It was also clear to me that we weren't ready to serve the fashion industry—that it would be much more appropriate to serve the retail yarn customer by selling to the knit shops. And that is how this business evolved into today being a line of yarn that we import and sell to yarn shops.

David: Really? Your travels have taken you from remote villages in Latin America to remote villages in Asia and Africa.

Susan: That's right.

David: I was in Morocco for a short visit, which could be described as interesting. I also think that a lot of people coming out of college find out that you can't duplicate the experience you get when you are actually visiting a place. It changes your whole outlook, like you said. Also, I had to think back to when we first met; we were introduced when the Sustainable Furniture Council [now Sustainable Furnishings Council] was formed. It was 2006, wasn't it?

Susan: It was. That's when we had that first organizational meeting.

David: I remember volunteering because I had done some consulting, well, sustainable manufacturing consulting, really. I thought that I could be of service. That's when I first met you. Can you give me sort of the timeline or the narrative of the evolution of SFC? And you, now, as the executive director, have been successful in gaining membership and establishing consensus, which is never easy.

Susan: In September of 2006, I was working with my From the Mountain business, putting more and more products in the home furnishings industry. I got wind of the fact that there was a meeting planned to start a sustainable furniture council and it was going to be in the South Cone showroom, Gerry Cooklin's showroom. I showed up for that and it was an all-day event that Daphne Hewitt [Rainforest Alliance] moderated, featuring speakers including Lou Newitt [Knoll], Amy Chender [ABC

Carpet and Home], Penny Bonda [USGBC and Ecoimpact Consulting], and Jamey French [Former Chairman, FSC–US, Northland Forest Products]. There were lots of different perspectives, as you remember. Gerry's own message there was that he thought this was a pretty important idea to pursue and he was too busy so he needed others to get involved. He and Amy Chender and I put our heads together to form another meeting. That became the organizational meeting that was held a couple of weeks later at High Point Market in Gerry's showroom. You and so many others were there. At that meeting, we formed committees. We formed a governance committee, a standards committee, and a marketing committee. We sallied forth to do our work. The members of these committees, the companies that were involved from the beginning, are involved in the home furnishings industry in various ways, as suppliers, manufacturers, retailers, designers, et cetera. By the spring of 2007, six months later, we were fully incorporated, and we had several dozen member companies and had an exhibit area at High Point Market. We got off to a galloping start. By the end of that first year, we had about 100 members. Now we have about 400 members. All these members are companies that have made their own commitment to sustainability and transparency and to continuous improvement. We as an organization make it our business to support them in fulfilling their commitments. We are an educational organization. We provide guidance, resources, educational programming, networking support, and marketing support. Companies do have to qualify for that, and fortunately we have a lot that do.

David: To follow up on that, it seems to me that SFC has made quite an impact on residential furnishings. From my experience on the residential side of the furniture market, there seemed to be a pretty big void in sustainability education. You had real leaders within it but you didn't have any consensus.

Susan: Yeah, right.

David: One of the things that impressed me is throughout the history of SFC is that you've been able to bring people together. I think that's a main theme of this book: reaching out and sharing. What advice would you give to someone who wants to get involved and doesn't know how or doesn't think they can make a difference?

Susan: I would say, start anywhere [laughs]. It doesn't matter where you start, it matters that you begin. There's a wonderful quote that I cannot remember [laughs]. Just begin, just begin. The first thing is really to believe that everybody makes a difference. That is so important because of the choices that we make all the time. It's more and more said that we vote with our dollars, and it matters what brand you buy, and it matters what we spend our resources on. It does matter, but it also matters what conversations we have. It matters how we show up in our communities, large, medium, and small, both in our professional communities and our geographic communities. The first thing is to know that you make a difference and you really can start anywhere. Sustainability is a wide umbrella. I do tend to worry about all the things that fall under that umbrella. At Sustainable Furnishings Council, we concentrate on the subjects, the themes, that we in the home furnishings industry think can have the most impact in the shortest amount of time. We concentrate on our contribution to the global climate crisis and on matters of poor indoor air quality, as well as other pollution and waste. These areas, and there are many we can do very simply, are where we tend to focus. But, all of it matters so any place you start is good news.

David: Right, I think that it's excellent that we're talking about these areas of sustainable products and furnishings because it does translate to all products.

Susan: Yes, exactly.

David: This book was conceived with the idea that all you who I've reached out to would answer the same question: if there were one green deed you would like to see heeded, implemented, and passed on, what would it be and why?

Susan: It would be to use your imagination and to pay attention so that you reduce consumption and increase reuse of everything that you do consume. Recycle everything. Everything can be recycled one way or another. Some things take a lot of imagination and a lot of awareness to recycle. It's that very simple maxim—reduce, reuse, and recycle—but it takes imagination to actually do any of those things in more than a cursory way.

David: Right, nature is the perfect recycler. I think we often have looked to other options instead of nature's example, which has contributed to environmental problems.

Susan: Yes, look to Mother Nature, good guidance.

David: It's the concept of biomimicry: using nature as the example for designing for the future.

Susan: Exactly. The most abundant natural resource on our planet now is our garbage. It's what we have thrown away, but there isn't really an "away" because it is somewhere. There are these huge patches [of trash] in the oceans, in the Pacific Ocean especially. It's important for us to realize that we have created the most abundant natural resource and we've got to learn how to use it.

David: I think when I started Olive Designs my approach was more like a bottom-feeding fish as an example. We have a lot of waste out there, so how do we put it back into the life cycle of a product? We've created a significant problem by blindly creating and consuming products.

Susan: Yes, we have.

David: I wanted to talk a little bit about the sustainable manufacturing training we both did in Indonesia in 2007 and 2008 with SENADA. That was a great experience for me. I got such a better understanding of what others in the world are saying and the issues they are facing. Indonesia, as we have both witnessed, is a very poor nation. You spent a lot of time in Jakarta, which I found to be both overpopulated and really quite polluted. But the struggles that Indonesians go through are so distinct from ours in the United States. Anyone who's not witnessed firsthand another culture would never understand why they do what they do. Why would the Indonesians choose to carve up Borneo and Sumatra to grow palm oil plantations? Unless you see the dire conditions that many Indonesians live in, you couldn't possibly understand. I know your experience was slightly different than mine. I was lucky to do my sustainable manufacturing training in Jogjakarta, in south central Java, which I greatly enjoyed. In my own way I was able to impart my knowledge of sustainability to these home accessory companies. And I learned as much as I gave. You had the opportunity to be there, what did you gain in terms of your experience from being in Indonesia?

Susan: I loved being in Jogja [Jogjakarta]—it was my favorite part of being in Indonesia too and working with the same sorts of businesses. One of the important things about the work on that project and other similar projects that I've done in other parts of the world is to let communities know that there are other ways to make a living other than cutting down your forest and converting to palm oil. Why would they want to convert to palm oil? Well, because there is a ready market for that product. The important thing to do is to point out that the world is full of other ready markets also. Then the challenge is to ensure that the artisan entrepreneurs get as much value for their effort, as much value as possible added to their communities where they work and live, which does not happen with the palm oil plantations. Much more is lost in all measures, not just in biodiversity but in the uneven distribution of all the profits from selling the products. They come from that palm oil or other commodity product, but they do not come back in value to those communities. That is an important thing to teach, to reveal, to emphasize—that the real success will be finding ways of generating income there that will stay there. That does happen in making best use of the resources at hand rather than doing away with any of those resources.

David: That's exactly what I was going to move on to because I've mentioned this part of my consultancy in other interviews for the book. I was able to go to Borneo and stay at an eco-lodge called Samboja in Eastern Kalimantan, which was one of the highlights of my consultancy. I got to witness Indonesians working together to support the eco-lodge, and gain knowledge of the importance of ecotourism. I wasn't expecting that and didn't know it existed there.

Susan: Ecotourism can often generate more money quicker than selling a handcrafted product whether you're selling it for regional markets or export markets. It can also tie into selling products, because the hospitality industry can buy many hand-carved soap dishes or something of that sort, in addition to tourists that love to buy handcrafted souvenirs and gifts to take home with them.

David: One thing that was really encouraging for me was to see the Indonesians developing a greater appreciation for ecotourism. I was trying to make that connection when I was doing my lectures stating that you couldn't possibly put a high enough price on the value of an orangutan. I know that SFC takes an interest in the logging practices of the home furnishings industry in these rain forest regions and in supporting the preservation of species. How did that come about?

Susan: Absolutely, we're very pleased to be involved in that effort. And it's an ongoing effort. There have been people trying to save the forest who have addressed the home furnishings industry for decades. I do think it's an area where we've been able to make some difference and partly by supporting the amendment of the Lacey Act in 2008. What is significant now is the expansion of the Lacey Act. It is a hundred-year-old law that after 2008 began protecting not only wildlife but also protecting plants. The amendment says it is against U.S. law to buy, sell, trade, or transport any plant product—including wood—that has reached its destination by breaking any laws at all. I'm very proud of that because the U.S. was the first nation to enact this. There is now a European Union law that does the same sort of thing. This means that we in the U.S. can enforce our laws such that other nations' laws are better obeyed.

David: More universally.

Susan: More universally, that's right. We've been very active in making sure this amendment to the law keeps its teeth. We're very proud to be part of the Forest Legality Alliance. I was just in Washington at WWF [World Wildlife Fund] last month for the meeting of that group. We talked about what's needed now for preserving forests around the world, and lots of other big NGOs [nongovernmental organizations] were also there. Recall that Rainforest Alliance and WWF helped get us started [at SFC]. Rainforest Alliance and WWF were interested in being involved when we got started because they knew, way before most people in the home furnishings industry knew, that we in this industry add the highest value to any wood resource. We are, of course, hungry for the best woods in the forest, so we are in a very significant position to save the forests of the world. We are a small industry, and we're a small industry of small businesses; it's very fragmented. Much of the furniture that goes into our homes and that is sold in furniture stores today is made of materials that have come from all over the world. It's mixed up and it's really difficult to track it. We know that the way that it's going to get easier is with consumers and interior designers and store buyers asking where the wood comes from, and if there's proof of origin.

David: And a label. The most stringent, the Forest Stewardship Council label, confirms that the manufacturer has gone the distance.

Susan: That's right. FSC is the best and most corruption-proof label for wood products.

David: The other ones are getting better. They're beginning to understand that they have to have more transparency in chain of custody. I know we speak in similar terms about sustainable products, and we both help to define what they are. What should consumers look for when shopping for home furnishings—for example, we mentioned the FSC label, but what else should they look for when shopping for sustainable furnishings products?

Susan: There are a few questions that I love to suggest that people keep in mind. The first one is, where is it made? Was it made anywhere near where you are? What was it made of—was it made of materials that come from anywhere near where you are? If you're here in North America and it's made in North America of North American materials, that's typically good news. We are a fairly law-abiding people for the most part [laughs], and we do have good environmental protection laws here, so if it is made here of North American materials, that's a good thing to look for. Of course, most of what you see in most stores that sell furniture—or anything else—is made elsewhere. Being mindful of what constitutes good materials is very important. We've talked a lot about garbage being our most abundant natural resource, so I'd love for people to know to look for recycled content and to know to look for a significant percentage of recycled content. There is in sometimes a tendency to say that a product has recycled content, but it's a minute amount of recycled content. Ask the questions. Dig a little bit deeper. Finally, what I'll say is be sure that you ask something about how this product is finished. We love new products. Most people do and they love the assurance that it is a new product because it has this new product smell, but as we know that new product smell is actually the smell of potentially harmful chemicals that are off-gassing.

David: Both wood and metal finishing can be very toxic.

Susan: Yes, they really can be.

David: Who are your environmental heroes, or where did you gain your inspiration?

Susan: I'll tell you both. The first person that came to mind when you ask about environmental heroes is Pete Seeger [1919–2014]. Not only because he did so much, like helping clean up the Hudson River, but because he sang. That is so much part of being my hero. I don't sing myself, well…I sometimes make a joyful noise but people don't want to hear that [laughs]. I do dance but that isn't sharing in the same sort of way. Singing and bringing voices together was such an important part of what he did. It so served the projects and the causes he worked on. He [Pete Seeger] is a real hero for bringing together voices and bringing them together in song.

David: For many, many decades.

Susan: He sure did. He passed away just last year. My son, Ripley White-side, is an artist and did a project on the recently deceased called R.I.P. that included Pete Seeger—I'll show you that before you leave too. My influences are my parents and my grandparents. We grew up on a farm that had been in the family for a very long time and that my brother now farms organically. The farm land was rented and farmed by a farmer down the road when I was growing up. When my brother left college, he decided he wanted to farm. He has been farming it organically for thirty-odd years now. He is another example of the influence of the way they raised us. We had this closeness to nature. I also mentioned my grandfathers: the one grandfather was Archdeacon of the Yukon, 1915 to 1925, and the other, who was a civil engineer, worked for the Royal Corps of Engineers and built railway systems all over the world. He got to know the languages where he lived and painted pictures of the scenes he was seeing so both those [men] are very influential bits of my heritage. The main thing is I grew up talking about this stuff—near lots of green and the outdoors.

David: As a kid, I imagine looking at those pictures of faraway places would put that in your mind.

Susan: It's true. The other thing as a kid was watching my parents be active in the community, with projects like saving a waterfront right there in the little town of Edenton and things like that. By being part of the collective voice that was saying "No, this would not serve us and everybody in this community."

David: Edenton is a very small place. It must be very special.

Susan: It's in the northeast corner of North Carolina. It's on the inland waterway on the Edenton Bay, which is a bay of the Albemarle Sound.

David: You certainly have been an inspiration to me. I'm sure you continue to inspire many, many people. You're a treat. Thank you.

Susan: Thank you, David, it's great to visit with you for your book. I'm honored to be a part of it.

CHAPTER 8

"They were traditional people, and I became friends with them, and they began to teach me."

Photo by Maryann Mahood

G. Peter Jemison

Native American Artist and Historian

Ganondagan

I've had lifelong empathy for America's Native peoples, specifically, those who resided in what is now the United States of America. Long before we white colonists discovered the wealth of resources that our newfound homeland contained, the original inhabitants had established a spiritual relationship with it. They well understood that their survival depended on being in tune with nature. Although Native American tribes were in conflict, and often displaced each other from their homeland, they never truly comprehended the idea of privatization and parceling of turf until it was forced upon them by white colonists. We have a long, ugly history of mistreatment of Native Americans here in the United States. I was first exposed to this when I was in my early teens and read the bestseller, *Bury My Heart at Wounded Knee*.[1] It made a profound impact on me and despite some of its inaccuracies (I learned later), it still is a key book, and one of the best ever written, in understanding the conquest of Native Americans. I first learned about the Iroquois (or Haudenosaunee, their Native name) in Gary DeBolt's social studies classes in high school in Geneseo, New York, a town that lies within what was once the homeland of the Seneca Nation—the Western Doorkeeper of the Haudenosaunee. The most powerful of the Six Nations, the Seneca, were decimated by the Revolutionary War, as all of the Haudenosaunee were.

Fractured by split loyalty to the Colonist Army and the British, no tribe was caught more in the crossfire of the war, and after the surrender at Yorktown, the only promise kept to them by either side was their removal and loss of ancient tribal lands. The consequence of being in the wrong place at the wrong time was that they would have to "negotiate" a form of peace, which was equivalent to giving up their home.

The Haudenosaunee had settled in some of the most awe-inspiring natural areas of Western New York. From the Adirondack Mountains to Lake Erie, encompassing all of the Finger Lakes, which still are referred to by their Native American names, these regions of breathtaking beauty comprised their tribal homeland. From a natural resource viewpoint, the Six Nations had a lot to lose. Their ability to embrace communal living through concepts that included traditional longhouses, as well as their protocol for all six tribes to be represented in council, made them one of the most formidable and socially and culturally advanced Native American tribes in American history.² However, treaty making with avaricious and deceitful white settlers proved their undoing, as it did many other tribes. The English phrase *Indian giver* to describe someone who takes back a gift is not only paradoxical but disturbing to me.

Peter Jemison is a member of the Heron Clan of the Seneca and a Seneca Native from both sides of his family. He is the eighth-generation descendant of one of the more remarkable members of the tribe: Mary Jemison, or the "White Woman of the Genesee." Captured in her teens by French and Shawnee Indian raiders during the French and Indian War, she was one of only two spared. Her parents and most of her siblings were tortured and scalped. The raiding party sold Mary to a Seneca family who had also endured a family loss. Ultimately, a widowed Mary Jemison settled along the Genesee River with her Seneca family and became an accepted member of the tribe. Rearing a number of children, including Peter's direct descendant, Thomas, Mary lived a long, fascinating life as an adopted Native American or Seneca, until her death at 90 in 1833.³ She is forever memorialized by a gorgeous bronze statue in her ancient homeland deep within Letchworth State Park in western New York very near where I was raised.

Interview—2016

I had discovered Peter's work through my continued interest in Native American history and cultural centers. I had never met Peter before, which is a departure from all other chapters, but I didn't feel I could write this book without hearing from a Native American historian and cultural preservationist. He is a well-known Native American artist, who has shown his work around the country, as well as curated other Native art exhibits. He is a writer, artist, historian, documentarian; he even went back to get another degree, a master's in American Studies, from SUNY Buffalo, later in life. His circuitous path led him to become the site manager of Ganondagan, which is the former location of the largest Seneca town in the 1600s. It is a New York State historic site that includes a Seneca cultural center and museum, theater and auditorium, a restored bark longhouse, and 17,000 square feet of land complete with replanted traditional grasses and plants that can be seen along various hiking trails.

On May 9, the day after Mother's Day, I met Peter at Ganondagan, north of Geneseo, in the town of Victor. The visit to Ganondagan was a family outing since both of my parents, as well as Maryann, joined me. The center was officially closed, but Peter thoughtfully accommodated us all, including opening his small, unpretentious office within the cultural center to conduct my interview—and the cultural exhibit to enjoy while we spoke. As an aside, let me add that the cultural center is a remarkable building in many respects: the exhibits are vibrant, carefully laid out, and touching. I was quickly reminded of the Museum of the American Indian in Washington, D.C. It reflects on the Seneca in such a moving way. One comes out of there feeling the spirit of a proud culture. A culture that owes a debt to a wise elder, Peter Jemison, who I had the honor of speaking with that day.

David: I think the idea of being able to preserve this area, and the long struggle that you went through to get this open, is pretty exceptional. Explain how you came to this site, and what brought you to it. How do you preserve some of the traditions at the Center?

Peter: Well, back in 1984, I had been living in New York City at that point for about seven years. I was running an art gallery showing Native contemporary artists. I was living in Lower East Side Manhattan and the gallery was in SoHo. We were having good success. It was very difficult. It didn't have a lot of staff. It was really a one-man show. There were a lot of volunteers that would come and help me. Anyway, I had burned out on New York. My cousin told me about a job opening here. He very briefly described it. I had some awareness, not a lot, just a little, that there was a Seneca historical site here. They'd been having meetings and discussing how they might interpret it and what they would do with it. In the end, I decide to apply for the job. To make a long story short, I got the job. Then I came here, and relocated myself from a five-room apartment in New York City. Here it was a whole different setup; it was over 200 acres of land with a ten-room house. But the condition of all the buildings was terrible. It was an abandoned farm and collapsing old farm buildings. The house was not inhabitable at the time, and had to be renovated. I really started questioning myself, *What have I done? My God, how long is this going to take to even begin to be something that people would want to visit?* There was a plan that was being implemented. They had received two different National Endowment for the Humanities grants, which included signage, a film, publications, a master plan and so forth. I had a group of all Native consultants who were working with the Bureau of Historic Sites of New York State Parks. I would begin by meeting with them discussing the master plan, learning more about the site. But I really had to take a crash course. Which, I did, for myself, and others directed me to go back into the seventeenth century and really learn what the history of contact was between French and Seneca and Dutch and Seneca and English and Seneca and English and the Haudenosaunee, and how that all is going. It was a quick learning experience.

Gradually over time I began to get a handle on it, and of the many, many stories. Not too long after I got here—maybe four years—I formed a Friends organization: The Friends of Ganondagan. We were all volunteers and people who had an interest in the site and people I knew, a few anyhow, but most of them I was just meeting for the first time. It just went along for a while like that. There were hiking trails, school visits, a converted small building that was used for a visitor center. It was mainly an outdoor site. We were open six months out of the year. We'd open in May and close at the end of October. Then I started reaching out to more and more schools and working with staff—that kind of thing.

Then my cousin said to me, "I think you should go back to school and pick up a master's. It will help to cement your credentials." I had an undergraduate degree. But he said, "I think you should go back to UB [SUNY Buffalo], pick up American Studies, get a master's." So, I went there, which was a good move. It gave me a good perspective on the history and so forth. That was a good move. The first thing I really initiated and made happen was the building of a bark longhouse. The fourth graders coming here were standing in the middle of a field looking at an 1800s building or two. Then, looking at modern buildings—twentieth-century buildings—it's so hard to imagine a bark longhouse, you know? They didn't have the scale. They were building tiny models in their classrooms.

That took quite a fight. To get people to accept the idea that we could take something that did not exist. There was almost no remnant of it. The footprint that was left was something you couldn't really interpret. I had to find a Seneca bark longhouse that had been excavated and use that. The mapping of the post molds, to be able to say, "This building has an authentic footprint anyway." Finally, a company was familiar with building a bark longhouse, and we contracted with them and raised the money for that. Then we took that and we actually created a film around the building of it. We had a guide for teachers to work from. That really began to draw. It was an attraction. Especially an attraction for students to be able to come and see an authentic bark longhouse. Then, we had the furnishings of it and the making of things that were Native, that were in there, along with purchasing trade items that people were making again and having those for sale. We did a whole thing on learning about the fur trade system; learning about the building of the longhouse. I always said it became a teaching tool for us. It opened up so many ideas and so many things that we just never thought about before. That was helpful. Gradually I got to thinking about this new building.

Trying to figure out how it would be done, because I knew it would be a lot of money that would have to be raised. I had people come to me who were interested in the idea. They had suggestions and some of their ideas were good but I couldn't accept the whole idea they had. Way back in 1990, I got involved with repatriation [Native American Graves Protection and Repatriation Act of 1990]. This law that was passed allowed us to bring back human remains for the purpose of a proper burial, as well as sacred objects, objects of cultural matrimony from museums. I became the head of that for the confederacy, excluding the Oneidas—they worked independently because there are two Oneida nations. I worked for the Senecas, Cayugas, Onondagas, Mohawk, Tuscarora. We brought back lots of our ancestors and lots of important things. Some of the people who had a vision for this building wanted me to create a mausoleum, literally where the remains would still be housed in the building. Artifacts would be on another floor, contemporary exhibits, perhaps. I just had a commitment to burying the remains. I had to work towards that. That's really what our people wanted. They wanted that to happen. But again, it put me in touch with a variety of people.

Again, my background being in art and being a curator and so forth, I had another opportunity to work with the Fenimore Art Museum in

Cooperstown, to begin to mount biannual exhibits of contemporary artists and the like. That put me in touch with another philanthropist who liked my work and was interested in what I was doing. That became my pattern. When I found people that understood what I was doing, that I didn't have to convince about it, I would spend time working on getting their support, working out details with them on how they would support the project, looking a little bit at other sources for funding, my own Nation and others. It was a lot of really going back to people that I had met years before in some connection that I had with them. A Native-owned company from Ithaca, I had known the founder many, many years ago. I was really fortunate, too, that I had a commissioner that when I said that I want to build a bark longhouse, and I took her into the New York State museum and I showed her a partially recon-structed bark long house. She was like, "We need to get you 125,000 dollars so you can get started." I was like, "Yes, now you're talking my language." I don't want to talk about things; I just want to do it. That, of course, was the seed money that brought other money together. She was always that way, if I talked to her. She took me one time and she said, "You have to serve on the Advisory Counsel in Historic Preservation." This is a presidential appointment, I mean, you have to be vetted by the White House. I had just accepted another position on the board for the American Association of Museums.

I said, "You know, these two things overlap." Each of them has quar-terly meetings; each of them has an annual meeting; each of them asks you to do all this other work independently at times. And I said, "Now you're giving me another one? I have a full-time job!"

She said, "Well, you got to do it. You're the only one I trust."

"OK," I said.

She said, "Don't worry about the expenses. The government pays for those. You just do the work."

I said, "You owe me one [laughs]. One big one." In the end she helped me raise $1,700,000. That really, again, got the project going. Got the project started.

The philanthropist who I worked with [the exhibits] came in and said, "I'll fly my jet from New Mexico. I'll pick up this other group of people that I want to have support this. I'll fly them up to a meeting here in Rochester. I'm going to give a million dollars to the project and we'll see what they'll do."

Again, to somebody like that you just say, "Thank you, that's fantastic" [laughs]. All of those kinds of things can fall in place. At the same time, I started thinking about the landscape. I had been down to the Falling Waters in Pennsylvania. I like the fact that they were managing the environment around that beautiful structure. I thought, *That's what I want to do here. I want the landscape to be a managed landscape. I want to return some of it to the way it looked in the 1600s when people lived here. Let's reintroduce native grasses; that'll be a part of the view that people will see.*

I had a notion where the building would be sited. In the end, we had to move it, but we still put the native grasses in, and that, to me, really added a very interesting element to the landscape. I had a cousin named John Mohawk who had started a project to take our heirloom corn and make it available to our community. To take that corn also out to the public and get it to high-class restaurants, food providers, and so forth. He passed away unexpectedly—he had been the one convincing me to get the degree in American Studies. Anyhow, I knew all of the equipment was sitting in a log cabin over there on his property. I went over there and talked to the one surviving relative that was taking responsibility. We bought the equipment and moved it back here and established the project here. It's called Iroquois White Corn Project. We process our heirloom white corn, and we buy it from one of our local Native farmers. We produce three products: we produce a roasted white corn, a white corn flour, and a whole hulled corn that people can use for soups and salads. We sell that as well as we provide it back to our community. We sell it to our community and we sell it the greater public. We have a regional distributor who gets it out there. Wegmans [grocer] carries it down in Ithaca and over here in Canandaigua, and we got Hart's Market in Rochester that's carrying it—not all the Wegmans do. Anyway, it was to bring a stream of income to the Friends' organization. All this time I'm still working on pulling together the building money. I had seen a building up in the Adirondacks that was built for about fifteen million. So, my goal was fifteen million. That's what I was going for. If we raised more, that'd be good, but I'd at least have to have that much. But it took convincing. It took me to convince my Nation about that idea, New York Parks and

Recreation about the idea, and the philanthropists were in and out and came back again. The thing about the building was that we started off saying that we'll go for a LEED green building rating. A LEED Gold or Silver rating. Something that didn't cost so much to build that we couldn't recoup the benefit. We went with geothermal [energy source] in the end, and did a lot with the windows too as far as weather proofing, and we did other things too. The whole project, the total project, came in at fifteen million. The Friends' organization managed the money that came strictly for the building, which came from the philanthropists. The state managed the state-funded money. We had two separate pots of money, and they couldn't be comingled. That was the interesting part. If you took state money, it had to be everything outside of the building. Or things that we could contract for that had to be brought into the building. Otherwise, we had to pay for things with the Friends' money that they were managing. We had a retired bankruptcy court judge who was becoming a member of the Friends and became the person in charge with the purse strings. He was an excellent money manager. We stayed within budget; in fact, we came in under budget. I had an architect that I was kind of wedded to, and I had architectural firms who were friends of mine, who helped me in the initial stages to create interest by doing a lot of pro bono work and creating drawings and so forth. Finally, I was able to work it out so that two of them worked together. One designed it and then one was the architect of record. They figured out how to value engineer it so we could build it for the money that we had. They were a great local outfit. The architect was already in his eighties, so he was no competition for the younger fellow, but more of a help to get him through the process. The other architect had a small shop, and they worked together. We had other local guys who really gave us a lot to make it work, as well as a pipe company out of Rochester that was a good construction management team. Things come together and you're learning all the time about stuff that you didn't know anything about really. I never built a building before.

David: Do you ever feel like you're the only person that could have done this? You had your own expertise, all these contacts, people who are willing to work pro bono—who else could have done this?

Peter: I don't know. I've had people tell me that "no one could take over your job. They're going to be able to take over one part, and somebody else does this part, and somebody else takes this part, but nobody else has the experience or the contacts that you've got." It's a lifetime of learning and living with people that brought me to this point. Sometimes it was a combination of luck and a combination of doing the right thing. I knew what I was trying to do, and you have these connections, but at times you have to have the guts to do it, have the guts to say, this is what I need. It may sound outrageous but it may not sound outrageous to some people, and they may just say, "Oh, we can do that. That's nothing." I found out what I could do that way.

David: Yesterday, we were just out at the old council grounds of Letchworth [Letchworth State Park]. Obviously, you're also a historian of your people as well. Eight generations removed from Mary [Jemison]. You were telling me you were eight or nine when you first became aware of that.

Peter: We used to have pageants on the lawn in Letchworth State Park telling the story of her capture and adoption and her settling there. Her eventually marrying a Seneca—she married a Delaware first when she was young. We were sitting on the lawn watching this pageant. This was the first time I heard anybody mention Jemison, Jemison, Jemison. I said to my Dad, "Why don't you tell them we're here? We're probably the only Jemison's here."

He goes, "No, no. I don't want to do that." He didn't want to draw attention to us, and he didn't say anything. It registered in my mind that this was our story. Even though it was a long way back, this was the person we descended from. In my community, there were Jemisons, Jimmersons, Jamisons. I grew up in a Seneca community so I knew all these people and met others along the way whose names were spelled a little different. Everybody would say they all eventually come back to her. So then when I came here to work, I had lots of people coming to me. They had read Mary Jemison's book, and they were knowledgeable about it. They would ask me about how I was connected to her. "How are you related to her?" Well, my father knew five generations back but he didn't know those last three. He didn't have any real handle on that. I went to a genealogist who used to work at one of the colleges in Fredonia. He did the genealogy for me and showed me how I was related to her. So now if I went out to talk to people, I could explain it, I understood it.

Then my father passed on and I became the executor of the family estate on the Cattaraugus reservation. Now I really got to know who my relatives were again because of the family and the land issue. In the meantime, a number of years back, I had gone to work for the Seneca nation but I didn't know my mother's side of the family. My mother's family came from Allegany [reservation] and my father from Cattaraugus. I knew a little bit of my mother's family—I knew her immediate sisters—but I didn't know the rest of the family. Once working for the Nation and running programs on the Allegany and the Cattaraugus, I really got to meet all of my mother's side of the family, and they took me in. They were really quite kind to me and patient with me. Then because of the work that I was doing, I got to know all these people who were really the ones that maintained what we call our way of life. They were singers; they were dancers; they were artists, and fluent speakers, craftsmen, cooks, and all these different things and traditions. They were traditional people, and I became friends with them, and they began to teach me. They would make me feel a part of it. They were always bringing me into things, involving me. Again, I felt blessed just to have found my way back home again and get all these things shown to me and be exposed to all these things. Later on, they become very valuable, so when you go someplace people know who you are. You don't have to stand there trying to win them over; they already know you.

David: I grew up in Geneseo and I knew some of the Seneca history, even learning in seventh grade that my hometown was traditional homeland of the Seneca. What do you think all these years later of the area and how it's been handled and maintained in terms of the environment? We haven't always been so good at developing the land and taking care of it. What do you think about how we've settled the area?

Peter: I've really had to deal with development. I've had to deal with a salt mine down at Hampton's Corners [New York] because I was doing the repatriation work because there were human remains discovered. I got put right in the middle of that—that whole controversy I had to deal with. I had to deal with the state, the governor's office, the owners of the mine, my Nation, people who were protesting the thing who were not Native. They were all taking shots at me because some of our people trespassed on that land because they heard what was going on and were upset by it. I also hold myself responsible because I should have brought them into the process sooner. What happened was that they wouldn't allow anyone else on the land except me. Now, I became the person who had direct contact with them in negotiations. What they didn't know, whoever it was, made it up, and I had to deal with a lot of stuff that wasn't true and try to fight that, fight against that kind of portrayal of the situation. It's crazy because recently they went back to development, doing some more things, and I got a chance to meet with them again. Different crew, different owners, but same story though. They hated that bad publicity they got; they didn't want any more of that. They wanted to start out on the right foot this time instead of doing things and then pulling us in. It was such a different story than the first time around, and I did have other people involved early on. It went better, you know. I've had to deal with development from Pennsylvania to West Virginia to New York to Ohio. I've had to deal with things that impacted our traditional lands. Some people understand and some people don't. Some people don't give a damn what I think, and they're going to do what they're going to do. Our needs are not theirs. I've had all those experiences. I've had others where when you're put into a leadership role you have to make decisions. When you make decisions, some people don't agree with you, and then you've got to deal with that. We have an expression and concept that our real leaders develop a skin that is seven spans thick. I've developed that. I now have that skin that's pretty thick. I can deal with it. I don't enjoy it but I know from experience what I have to do. After a while when you know what to do, it makes it easier because you're not second-guessing yourself. You know what you're supposed to do.

David: I have a friend from the Lakota Nation who is still trying to get the Black Hills back. That's very difficult.

Peter: It doesn't change. Sometimes it gets worse as time goes on.

David: One of the things I know that is important to you, actually a big part of this book, is the whole concept of giving awareness to other species, treating other species with respect. I know the term Orenda is important to you personally from your art but also from your tradition. Can you explain that a little bit?

Peter: We recognize that we believe in a creator. The creator made this world that we occupy. Things were placed here and they were given their way of living. They were given their instructions on how they were supposed to live. They used that instinct, knowledge, whatever you call it. I see reasoning even in there. They use that in order for them to survive. We humans tend to think of them as being there but without any real consciousness. We [Haudenosaunee] don't really think of it that way. We think in terms of, these are our relatives, and these relatives have provided for us. Some of them have literally given their lives for us to survive. Some of these relatives bring forth gifts that make it possible for us to survive.

Therefore we have to look at ourselves in terms of the big picture, in terms of the whole and where do we fit in there. We can be very destructive. We can be very damaging, or we can try to live in harmony with this world around us, try to be respectful of it and extend that thinking to other people, to those who are willing to listen to it—the ideas. So that concept of Orenda is that every living thing has a spirit, and you are just a part of the bigger, bigger picture. Sometimes you know I have managed to put myself into situations where I've experienced a kind of magic that is a part of a spiritual belief, I guess you could say. When you encounter it, you feel very fortunate. That what you believed you've actually seen revealed to you. That is living with a consciousness—placing yourself within the world around you in a way that you're open to it. You're open to the feelings, the sounds, the sights, and all the rest to go with it. So that's me. I've been awfully lucky with the kind of teachers that I've had. They took the time to teach me, whatever time was necessary. Once I earned their respect, for them to teach me what I needed to know, they never looked at it like "I don't have the time." They looked at it like "You're worthwhile, and I'm going to help you understand and learn, and I expect you to act according to that. You'll go out and do whatever you're going to do. You're going to keep this understanding going by sharing it."

David: That's exactly what the concept of this book really is: one good action generates another. If you had one green deed you'd like to see heeded, adopted, and passed on, what would it be? That's the same question I've sought answers to from everybody in the book. Of course, putting that back on you, you may likely have just answered it: that consciousness.

Peter: It is that consciousness of your place in this world. Part of it has to be, but unfortunately it takes a lifetime to gain that, that full understanding of it. If you start off with the idea that you are a conscious person, you are a person with the power of reasoning, and that you can learn and enjoy what you learn and witness—then it's not just a process that you enjoy, it's a process you love. It's a process where you experience the rewards of being that way. So, whatever it takes to open that lid in somebody and let in the information that they're ready for at that time that can be built upon. I've told some young people this: "You may only hear this once in your lifetime. It could be I may be the only one to say this particular thing. You have to take what I tell you and you add it to all the other experiences you're going to have. All of that will then help to fill out who you are and what it is, what it means, to say that I'm a Seneca. What it means to say Ongwehonweh—meaning 'I'm part of the original people.' When you do that, you realize how really special it is that you've been born into this particular group of people. Not that other people aren't capable of it, but this is where we come from. This is the part of the world we know about, that we've been shown, and we've lived in. Now, you're going to learn too. You're going to carry it on, I hope you [young people] will anyway."

One of those things is just extending love toward people, toward young people, younger than yourself, so that they will feel you care about them. You want them to know there's somebody that cares about them, somebody that's willing to share and teach them things, whatever that may be. Just being kind. Showing somebody kindness is possible so they don't always encounter negativity or people looking down at them for whatever reason. They are a good person, fundamentally. Some of them need a lot of work; some need some shaping. Some of them have failed and gotten back up. We've dealt with them all. When I say we, I mean my wife and I. We took into our home about eighteen different young people who have stayed with us for periods of time. Some stayed with us, are still with us. Some have spent whole high school years with us. Some were there for just a few months. They asked to stay—they came to us and asked if they could stay. One needed to get away from a gang. Basically they would have killed him if he went back to them or if he didn't go back to them, so he couldn't go there. We extended ourselves to them and tried to help them out. Some didn't make it, and some haven't made it all the way. Some are still going, still doing their thing; still learning and still growing.

David: You're carrying on that legacy of kindness?

Peter: Yeah, a legacy of kindness; a legacy of caring; a legacy of teaching—of showing them another way that they could be as a human. And that will, we hope, make the world a little better. In a small way, a little bit better.

David: And this place has got to be a sense of healing for your Nation.

Peter: I got an award here on Friday—Friday morning—a "legacy award," they called it. The people who came, not Native, they were just thanking me for doing this work. Thanking me for having the perseverance to see it happen and saying what an accomplishment and all that because they think it adds to this region, that it brings something to the region that is so unique. You realize that yes I have two different groups of people: there's my own Native people, my own Seneca people who I hope will come and discover for themselves things they didn't know, and then there's all the rest of the people out there who also have that opportunity. They'll receive it according to where they're at and what they understand. Then, you feel this was worthwhile, and that nothing else compares, not the time it took nor the struggle that may have been involved, because it was worth it. It was worth it.

David: Like I said before, you're probably the only one that could have pulled this off. You did a great job. I'm excited about this chapter for the book because I wanted a Native American perspective. What place better than the place where I grew up? My parents are historians so they're well aware of all the treaties and all the deception and rum bottles, and whatever.

Peter: The treaty [Treaty of the Big Tree] is quite a smear on everybody. There's a sign right there in Geneseo—it's unbelievable [sighs]. The last thing I'll say about that is: I look at those situations and I say to myself, *Given the things I've been through, how would I have handled it? If I had been there at that time, could I have been bigger than that? Could I have been able to* *stay out of the things other people got trapped into and felt forced to do?* I have real sympathy for people who were in those circumstances.

David: Divide and conquer. That's how they got those treaties done. Divide and conquer, and a lot of deceit and greed. It's not unlike most of the treaties that were signed.

Peter: One last story. Since before the 200th anniversary of the Canandaigua treaty in 1992, I had already been commemorating it, organizing it, bringing people in, and putting a book together. You put your belief into something that has had so many violations to it, yet realize that it still has power. It still has power. The twenty-seventh of February we went to a meeting at the state department in the old executive office building in Washington, D.C. The whole thing came about because of a treaty exhibit at the National Museum of the American Indian. The very first treaty that was featured was the Canandaigua treaty [Canandaigua Treaty of 1794]. They brought over the original treaty from the national archives and put it on exhibit there. That led to a meeting with the president; it led to a meeting with the state department. And we'll see where it goes from here. When somebody tells me to forget about that stuff—that it was 200-some odd years ago—I can't. For you that's past tense but for us we're living it right today. We're right in the same place living it still today, and so we have to insist that this is what you said in words. In your own constitution [U.S. Constitution], it says treaties are the supreme law of the land. We have to hold you to that. We have to ask you to live up to the words of your presidents and founders.

"No matter where you are, sustainability should be creating a better experience."

Photo by Maryann Mahood

Dina Belon

Green Buildings

Green Lifestyles

Hotel Tree Hugger

Dina Belon became my friend almost instantly upon introduction. After years of spontaneous meetings and informal discourse, I've developed a pretty keen sense of true environmental compassion, which is more a noble motivation driven by goodwill and good intentions. Dina struck me this way from the onset. Not only did she become my confidant in sustainability for NEWH, the hospitality network organization I've oft referenced, but she and I have always seemed to be in tune. While most of our interaction has been focused on greening the hospitality industry, we've shared our sentiments on sustainable living, preserving biodiversity, global climate change, and just about every affected issue in between (what else is there). I was fortunate to have overlapped with Dina in my service to NEWH because it has become a lasting friendship. I've attempted to share what I know and what I've helped create during my time as V.P. of Sustainable Hospitality for NEWH because that is the essence of sustainability. Dina was trained as a designer, which has far more relevance to greening hotels and restaurants than Spanish and international relations, for sure. But since that initial bond between us was genuine environmental concern, it has lasted for close to a decade. When I first met Dina in Orlando, Florida, in 2008, she and Trisha Poole, the NEWH Sunshine Chapter President at the time, as well as Vice President of Marketing for NEWH, Inc., were putting together a sustainable hospitality program and they invited me to speak. That day, I did my version of an *Inconvenient Truth* (Academy Award–winning documentary of 2007), entitled "What's Goin' On?"[1] I had just completed my consultancy in Indonesia so I was able to use some of my material from that incredible experience, which included real clarion-call images and statistics: for one, Jakarta had smog days where you couldn't see across the city on a sunny day, which I witnessed firsthand, and respiratory deaths overall were on the rise in Asia.[2] The hospitality industry, as an arm of tourism, is a big consumer of natural resources. Dina had begun her campaign to educate others on the monumental impact that buildings, including hotels, have on the environment. Green building practices have been in place for several decades now but hotels and restaurants have been slow to adapt. Dina's firm provided turnkey services for hospitality projects. Dina earned her LEED Accredited Professionals status before I had and was a good resource for me when I sought mine. That goes back to that sharing thing I talked about. In my opinion, the sustainability movement could be far more advanced if we shared more and sparred less. After that first meeting, I championed her efforts. Soon thereafter, Dina took on additional roles within NEWH, including Director of Sustainable Hospitality and finally succeeding me as V.P. of Sustainable Hospitality, which meant she would also serve on the Executive Committee. During our four years in tandem on the NEWH Board, we grew the national committee and accomplished about as much as any volunteer committee can. Any volunteer-based organization is as difficult to manage as a herd of ocelots—if there are any left by the publication of this book. We did our best to cajole, motivate, and inspire the hospitality industry into embracing green practices as a standard. The tide certainly began to turn as consumer demand for greener hotels increased.

Interview—2015

Dina joined Paladino and Company in early 2015, which expanded her focus to include commercial buildings and other markets, and ended her leadership of the NEWH Sustainable Hospitality Committee. Lamentably, I haven't had much exchange with Dina since her move to Paladino. I had known of their company and founder, Tom Paladino, since my early days at Olive Designs. They've been green building pioneers as a result of Tom's sustainability expertise and maintain an excellent reputation in the industry, so I was fully in support of Dina's decision to join Paladino in Seattle. It did require her family to relocate from the picturesque setting of Bend, Oregon. It also posed a challenge for me to schedule a sit-down interview due to our opposing coastal cities: Seattle and Beverly, Massachusetts. We contacted each other a few times after her move to Paladino and Company. Her career move broadened her activities, including her participation in green commercial shows like GreenBuild 2015. USGBC's GreenBuild is the annual conference for green buildings, which changes venues each year and attracts the industry's leaders. These shows bring 30,000 attendees and the most in-demand speakers on the subject in the world. I attended several in the past, and if there is one green show to be at, it's GreenBuild. The conjoining of youth, technology, scholars, and practitioners would move the most dispassionate scientist and spark that hope I have for us all. GreenBuild in 2015 was held in November in Washington, D.C. Dina and I agreed to meet the evening of the first night of the three-day event. It made logistical sense only because she was east of the Mississippi. Maryann and I knew that we'd at some point need to pass through D.C. on our two-week driving adventure that included most of the Atlantic coast. On our return trip north, we met Dina at the Grand Hyatt D.C., near the event, where she was staying. She was sneaking a quick bite before the Paladino party that evening, and despite her hectic schedule, we were able to chat and catch up for the year. Dina Belon is not a household name but she could be, and if your interests are designing green structures, crafting green hospitality strategies, and exploring green life-styles, you may hear about her. I know that I wanted to hear from her again.

David: Seems to me the places we're building are getting more and more environmentally friendly. In your many years in the hospitality and commercial building marketplace, what do you think has been the most important influencing factor?

Dina: I think the most important factor that has been, and still is, is money. As unfortunate as that is, I think money makes the word go 'round. The more we orient our sustainability program towards the value and the benefit from a financial perspective, the more successful it is. As much as I'm a tree hugger and I believe strongly in the initiatives that we do from a global perspective and the benefit to the planet and to the people that we interface with, I also understand that if I'm going to get those things done I want to get done, then I have to put them in a way that the decision makers will approve and agree to them. I jokingly say that I'm a sustainability accountant. I spend a lot of time orienting ideas into pro formas [pro forma invoices]. For example, we have the idea of putting in a better mechanical system and there are some costs associated with that or we have an idea doing a double skin on a building so we can incorporate natural ventilation. Not only simple ROI [return on investment], but how we articulate in a financial way the benefit to the building owner of those specific strategies.

David: Have we ever been in a presentation where there wasn't a bean counter? Hey, if they're gonna call us tree huggers, then we can call them bean counters.

Dina: Right. CFO [chief financial officer] presentation is what we do a lot. A second most important thing, and I think this is the foundation of our friendship, are the leaders, those people who have been on the cutting edge of sustainability who have chosen to take the risk and not be followers. They are the ones who have created success for all who've followed. Those first LEED-certified buildings and those first Living Building Challenge projects—all of those first guys who were involved and engaged and believed in it enough to do it when no one had done it yet. Marriot doesn't do that; Hilton doesn't do that. The system or the idea or concept has to be well tested and proven for large companies to make those moves. Those guys who are on the edge, we all owe a big thanks to them.

David: Talk a little bit about the Living Building Challenge. Most people don't realize the extent of that program; it goes beyond what we are addressing as green buildings.

Dina: I think a lot of people lose, at the high level, the difference between LEED and the Living Building Challenge. LEED is very prescriptive. It is literally a checklist, a checklist in which you have to do very specific things to accomplish those items. The Living Building Challenge essentially says I don't care how you get there. I don't care about the process in which you use, but I want you to be a net zero energy building, for example. I want you to recycle all of your water; I want you to eliminate any red list chemicals inside the building. It draws a very clear and distinct line that is challenging but also has a latitude to accomplish the outcome the best way for your project.[3] A lot of developers have a good bit of frustration around LEED because it's so prescriptive. We're working on a planned LEED platinum project at Paladino right now that is an island in French Polynesia. It is challenging with LEED because it's a private island in the middle of the Pacific. It doesn't fit an urban, commercial real estate model. In retrospect—we started this project a couple of years ago—I wish we did Living Building Challenge because it would have allowed us a lot more latitude. We're getting the end result, we're just not doing it in the prescriptive way the USGBC wants it done. In some circumstances people might find Living Building Challenge to be easier. The result isn't easier but it's easier to maneuver it.

David: It adds in a far more creative element to the process.

Dina: It does! It allows the team to stretch a lot more and be a lot more innovative.

David: In fairness to LEED, you couldn't have put together a program that was so specific to an island nation.

Dina: No, of course not. The amount of money it would have taken for USGBC to prescribe a process for a rare project like that isn't sensible.

David: I know you've worked on a lot of hotels and restaurants [projects]. You've been in hospitality for a long time. Some of these properties have embraced energy efficiency as a means of being green. Do you think they've taken enough steps to truly balance out consumption and conservation? Do you have any examples of organizations you've worked with that are sterling examples of sustainable principles?

Dina: Yeah, I have worked with a lot. They are making progress. The hospitality industry as a whole, both hotel, restaurant, venue, in its broader sense, is definitely a lagging industry compared to others. In my role now at Paladino, I work in commercial real estate, office, higher education, and even industrial markets. We work in a lot of different sectors. I get a nice broad brush compared to my early career, or my whole career for that matter, which has always been in hospitality. I was so insular, I didn't realize how far behind we were. As a lagging industry, hoteliers and restaurateurs are starting to see the value from an operating savings perspective. I think they still are missing kind of a top-line value as well as the health and wellness piece. Also, maybe some of the mission-driven cultural values they could get out of sustainability—both their internal employees' and their stakeholders'—as a company. Interestingly, I was involved early in creating a nonprofit called Green Destination Orlando. It was born out of the USGBC. I was the chairperson for the hospitality committee for the Central Florida Chapter of USGBC. We developed this program that would help hoteliers improve their sustainability even if they didn't do the basics like recycling. At that point, they were so far away from LEED, and that leap from where they are to LEED Silver [lower tier of LEED certification] was so big. That was the idea of it. How do we create little pebble stones for them to get to a LEED certification state?

That's how it was started, and it became so popular and got so big that we ended up splitting it off and creating its own nonprofit. It continues today. I'm so proud of that. It was a lot of hard work and a lot of sweat and tears creating that nonprofit. We actually produced last year, a first ever, destination-wide sustainability report. It's an entire report of what you can experience as a visitor to Orlando from a sustainability perspective. Basically, from the moment you land at the airport to the hotel you stay in, the car you drive, the restaurants you eat at, the destination you go to—Walt Disney World, for example. How can you have a total sustainable experience in Orlando, and what are each of those pieces and parts doing to create that holistic feel?

That report was a benchmark for Orlando to grow from, and it also developed some goals around what they're trying to accomplish. Of course, I've since left Orlando. It was sad and hard to leave all my friends there, but it's still going strong. That's one of my proudest things in the hospitality industry—to leave a kind of legacy in a city like that.

David: A city dominated by tourism.

Dina: It totally is! From the fifty-five million people who visit Orlando every year, you can educate a lot of people about sustainable solutions in a short period of time when they're on vacation. Orlando is not thought of as a sustainable city. If we can do it there, and we can touch that many people, and then all those fifty-five million people who go back to their homes can touch somebody else. That's how you make a difference. That's kind of the goal. One of the things that was really cool we did with GDO [Green Destination Orlando] was a partnership with the Electrification Coalition out of Washington, D.C. We created the first pilot of their drive electric program. We helped implement "Drive Electric Orlando," which was putting out infrastructure for electric cars. Orlando has three hundred and fifty electric car charging stations around the city, and a good part of those were placed in tourism locations. Now you can rent an electric car and have a sustainable transportation experience. It's like adding another "ride" to your Disney vacation. You can charge your rental car right at your hotel. When I was the sustainability director at a hotel in Orlando, we put in a program that if you showed up with an electric car and you were staying there, you got free parking—normally it was twenty dollars a day to park your car in our garage, free valet and free charging. We were always trying to create incentive for people. There are some really cool things that came out of that.

David: How would somebody find that organization?

Dina: There's a website, driveelectricorlando.com, that tells you all about the program.[4] It shows you where all the charging stations are and the locations of the participating rental car agencies.

David: That's perfect—leading us to discuss electric cars. I'm still amazed by how much Tesla has stimulated the automotive industry and how the electric car market has been revitalized. We remember the documentary *Who Killed the Electric Car?* from years and years ago.[5] It's certainly not dead now, no, it's very much alive. Battery and energy conversion have now hit the home market with super strong battery packs and efficient inverters. Are we getting to a time when we'll be off the grid with our neighborhood cities and even regions possibly?

Dina: I think so. I think the combination of the electric car and the autonomous car is going to be the key element that will bring us there; I think it's going to happen faster than probably people can handle. Soon, in very urban centers you'll see lanes of the highway that are autonomous car only. They'll be all electric and you won't own a car. You'll just swipe your card like I do today when I go to charge my electric car. I plug it in and I swipe the little card and the little thing pops out and I plug it into my car. You'll swipe your card and a little electric car will pull up and you'll jump in and it will autonomously drive you to where you're going. You'll jump out and you'll go to your job. I think that will absolutely happen in my working lifetime and I'm not that young.

David: I think the stimulus is there.

Dina: I suspect that it will start first in the West Coast, most likely in California, probably in San Francisco.

David: The idea that Tesla's getting into homes and the fact that their batteries will service homes. Off the grid homes are seemingly more and more now a reality.

Dina: It's becoming regulatory, right? So Title 24 in California now states that by 2020, residential homes have to be built to a net zero standard.[6]

That is five years, barely five years from now. Commercial buildings will be built to a net zero standard by 2030. That's amazing.

David: We're forty years late but we're getting there. I think the idea that so many people have, whether it's become a result of a weather-related incident—they've lost power, grids have failed, et cetera—found ways to back up power with generators or battery packs and inverters. To me, it's only going to grow.

Dina: It really is amazing to think that today my car, sitting out in the garage, could reverse energy to my house when I lose power. Today, I don't have that infrastructure. When we lose power at the house, it's excruciatingly frustrating to know that I have ten kilowatts of energy sitting in my car that I could plug my refrigerator into so my food wouldn't spoil. I think by next year I'll have one of those battery packs in my house.

David: Well, obviously, Tesla is breaking down barriers.

Dina: It's reasonably priced, too!

David: Like we were saying earlier, in our time with NEWH, we were somewhat of the green watchdogs. We were the "greenies." We were called "tree huggers." Originally that term was a derogatory term. Nobody wanted to be called *tree hugger* or a *granola type* because it was really marginalizing you. Do you think being a self-proclaimed environmentalist, as you and I are, has hurt us with our business opportunities over the years? I do kind of feel sometimes at odds with the general businessperson who doesn't embrace sustainability. Do you feel that it's hurt your business or your career in any way?

Dina: You know, it's hard to know. I know I got patted on the head a lot and told, "That's really nice, Dina, but we're going to go to do this because it's cheaper." I do consider myself a pragmatic tree hugger [laughs]. I worked in corporate America long enough to understand the reality of how they think. I will use business principle to show the traditional thinker that sustainability is not only smarter but that it produces better financial outcomes. But there are certainly days that I've gotten on my high horse and I've probably turned people off because they didn't want to hear the whys and the what fors. They just wanted to know the bottom line. I do think people will definitely tune you out when you start talking about environmentalism. When I say I'm a sustainability consultant, I either get somebody looking over my shoulder trying to figure out how to escape the conversation. Or in the best scenario they ask, "What does that mean?" I can then articulate to them not only the value from an environmental and social responsibility perspective but also the value from a profit perspective. I work really hard to always accentuate the triple bottom line.

David: One of those says profit.

Dina: It does. I think some of us in the environmental movement forget that sometimes. We swing the environmental flag so much that we forget that there's a triple bottom line. It's not just about saving the environment. We do need to save the environment, but to be able to do that we also need to have a sustainable business from a financial perspective.

David: We're doing no one a favor if they go out of business trying to be sustainable.

Dina: I want them to succeed more than anybody does. I want a Proximity Hotel [LEED Platinum Hotel in Greensboro, North Carolina] for everybody. I want somebody to do sustainability because it was a really great business decision to make, not just because they're a big ol' tree hugger. And to succeed and financially have a very successful business to prove both can be done very well.

David: That leads me into the next question, which is the one the book was written around. The uniqueness of this project has always been to get everyone's perspective on the same question: if you had one green deed you'd like to see heeded, adopted, and passed on, what would it be and why?

Dina: It's probably the toughest question; it takes a lot of thought. There are many that pop into my head. Ultimately, what I'd like to see is communities everywhere come together and care about the future, not just today. I'll use Seattle as a positive example. Sustainability has a long history and cultural impact on the community. I think that we, as a city, as a concentration of people, believe it, and believe in the core values of sustainability. I just read recently somewhere in a survey that was done that concluded that the majority of Seattleites believe sustainability is an important measure and an important initiative for the city. That's amazing to me! Make the comparison to Florida where I lived for thirty years. That is a place where the governor is a climate denier, even as south Florida is having saltwater intrusion into their freshwater systems during weather and high tide events. Seattle is really focused on community resiliency; the culture in Seattle cares about the future and our ability to continue to enjoy and protect the beauty of the region and its resources, including salmon, which we all love.

David: It's only slightly behind coffee.

Dina: [Laughs] You're right, we do support our Starbucks. But that to me [community resilience] is the thing I wish every community could have. I wish people could believe it and internalize it. Again, I don't mean in a tree hugger way. That's why I use the word *resiliency* instead of maybe only *sustainability* because I think it takes people to another place. It makes them step back and look at more the big picture of who they are and where they live as a people. I think if we would all step back and see that, then we might be able to connect the dots between all communities and we would actually induce global change.

David: It may be easier to rally around when you think about resiliency. Sustainability is also about survival. As a city, you wouldn't necessarily be rallying around sustainability as a means of survival but when you think that an industry like salmon fishing is so critical to the region. Just like cod fishing was in New England. Not was, still is, but it certainly has gone through its trials. A region, a city, they have rallying points and sustainability has to be a rallying point. We don't have multiple economies that are going to survive. We can only have a sustainable economy.

Dina: You're absolutely right. I have said to people for years that sustainability is not about saving the planet. The planet will survive, FYI—the thing that won't is us. We will be eliminated from the planet. Mother Earth will get rid of us as the scourge that caused the problem. It is not about Mother Earth surviving. She will, don't worry.

David: You're here [GreenBuild 2015] on behalf of Paladino. One of the organizations you've championed over the years is USGBC. What kind of impact do you think the USGBC has had since the 1990s when it was formed? I've attended a couple GreenBuild events and they draw over 30,000 attendees. That's not your typical green product trade show. What kind of impact do you think USGBC has had over the years?

Dina: I think the USGBC has done exactly what their mission was: market transformation. They have turned the market a complete left turn. I don't know any organization that's done anything like that at that scale. I don't know anybody in the real estate business completely unrelated to sustainability that doesn't know what LEED certification is. And not just the term, but that they pretty clearly understand what it takes to make that happen. That is phenomenal considering that the nineties weren't that long ago. I think that the USGBC has made such a market transformation that it's almost become a commodity now. It's so common, and that's what they wanted. That was the goal to get them to be the norm. We've said for years, you and I have said this, that it would be great someday in the future if nobody needs us. You wouldn't need somebody that knows about sustainability as a specialty; it would just be the way we function. In some circles, that exists today. In Seattle, as a city on the cutting edge of sustainability, architects and design firms in Seattle, they don't need a specialist to tell them how to do a LEED silver project. They know how to do it; it's a function of their service. I think they [USGBC] have done exactly what they wanted. They created market transformation. I could not applaud them more for that. I think the LEED dynamic plaque is an interesting divergence from the current method.

David: Right, for the follow-up monitoring program.

Dina: Yeah, I think that's a neat new program for them to come out with, where you have ongoing monitoring of a building. It takes away the prescriptive methodology and utilizes actual results.

David: Which you didn't have to do three years ago.

Dina: Actually, delivering the results is a great change that USGBC has made. I think it will allow them to continue and thrive and move forward.

David: We've collaborated a lot. I know I've watched you successfully engage many people. We talked a little bit about it earlier. No one likes to be lectured or cajoled into being more environmentally conscious. You've always been a positive figure that way. How do you build goodwill and environmental passion in others?

Dina: I think often people feel guilty when they talk to you when you're an environmentalist or a sustainable person. They have this guilt-ridden element to their conversation. I think the most important thing people in our position can do is ease this guilt and let people off the hook. None of us are perfect. I'll tell you one of mine. I love a really good hot shower. It's one of my last remaining [environmental sins], like, *I shouldn't do that.* I should be really good about that but I absolutely love to stand in the hot shower. I tell people that story sometimes. I'll tell them that story if they are clearly having that guilt-ridden moment with me. I'm like, "Let me tell you some of the things that I still do that aren't good. I use my garbage disposal on occasion." They're like, "Really?"

I'll say, "Yes, I threw some compost in my trash the other day."
Then they'll say, "Oh, I don't feel so bad now."

David: We don't want to condemn other people for their activities. I'm a very water-wasteful dishwasher. I know it. Still, I think that you and I have been successful in collaborating on educating others. Most people want to learn, but a lot of people get frustrated because they don't necessarily know how to get engaged. You've been successful with a lot of your educational events and getting people engaged. That's truly a talent.

Dina: The other thing is, we have to make sustainability sexier. It's kind of a dry topic. We have to make it fun and interesting and engaging. We can't talk about energy efficiency and mechanical systems all day long. We have to connect it to people. We have to show how sustainability impacts their lives in a positive way, not esoteric, but that you're going to get a better experience. I talk to hotel people about this all the time. The misconception that sustainability and guest experience are at odds with each other is absurd. A good sustainability program improves the guest experience and should improve your experience at home and at an office. No matter where you are, sustainability should be creating a better experience. I think when you start to engage people around that, then they get excited and they feel like the conversation is interesting.

David: Let's finish up with this question. It's been an interesting question to ask people throughout this process, about how they got involved.

What inspired them? Were there people who specifically influenced their behavior? I talk about from early experiences with my parents to amazing people I've met who have reshaped my thinking. Who drove you or what drove you to become environmentally conscious?

Dina: I was born in Alaska and as a very young child my family traveled the U.S., Mexico, and Canada for a year in an Airstream trailer and a yellow Suburban [SUV]. We stayed at national parks and my mom homeschooled us kids. We had a poodle, too, I recall. We went from national park to national park and KOA [Kampgrounds of America] campgrounds. I still to this day pass KOA campgrounds and I get all excited thinking that I'm a child again and we're going to stop and I'm going to be able to get out and get in a pool or run around and I won't be in a car any longer. It was an amazing experience, and it made me connected to our parks and to our country and its natural state. I have always lived in rural communities or small towns, until my move to Seattle. The biggest city I've ever lived in until Seattle was Bend, Oregon. I think that very rural upbringing made me very connected to the planet, and then I got into development, I got into real estate development in the hotel industry. I remember working on a project early in my career. I was very young, a very junior person in a very big meeting. We were going to lop off the top of a mountain in Gatlinburg, Tennessee, to put a resort on top of it. I remember sitting there with my stomach knotting up, not really knowing why, just innately believing that it was a bad idea. Raising my hand and saying, "I'm sorry, shouldn't we tier"—I don't even know how I knew what this meant—"the side or do something different? Isn't the community going to have a problem with this?" Everybody just whipped around and looked at me like I had an alien on top of my head. That's when I realized that my job and my ethos were incongruent to each other. I continued to work in hospitality and development for the next ten-plus years but that was the moment, the spark, that prompted me to learn about sustainable development and understanding how to do it better and smarter in the right way. We can still get great economic end results and be sensitive to the community and sensitive to the environment as well. I'm really glad I had both experiences. I'll make everybody in your book feel better though. The project never got built. It was in acquisitions, and we never ended up buying it. The mountain did not get lopped off. All is good.

David: Of course it's been mined since.

Dina: [Laughs] Probably.

David: This is interesting because now your career basically has taken you to a firm strictly doing sustainability work. You're no longer in those meetings where you have to raise your hand and then somebody has to think about sustainability. It's embedded in what your organization does. You've evolved into that role. It's got to be rewarding to be able to talk about sustainability as a fundamental thing that your business does.

Dina: It really is. I took a very circuitous route to get to where I'm at. I'm so lucky that every day I get to do something good and feel like I'm making a positive impact and help companies be smarter. Statistically, companies that have strong, well-thought-out sustainability programs perform better financially.

David: I remember some of the early green events that I went to when I started Olive Designs; Paladino was already there. Other pioneering leaders as well.

Dina: Tom Paladino is really a godfather of sustainability. He was involved in the original development of the LEED program. Paladino has been the technical editor of the LEED manual since the very beginning. We've certified over 650 projects. The depth of knowledge that Tom has is amazing.

David: Throughout some of these interviews, I've been thinking about some of those pioneers. Back then in the mid-nineties one of the keynote speakers was Ray Anderson, and think what he did for the industry. We all hearken back to those days when you had somebody who was willing to risk it all on sustainability like he did. From that point forward, we were all catching up.

Dina: He's the epitome of one of those leaders I mentioned at the beginning: those people that showed us all that it could be done well. One of the things that I loved about Ray's message the most was how he talked about it as a business imperative and a financial positive as a business owner. He believed in it very strongly, but he also knew other business owners would understand that language better. He was an inspiring guy to all of us.

David: We remember the year he passed. We did that environmental conference, and I got to share my past experiences with Ray. We were also able to show that wonderful tribute to him that included other environmental pioneers like Paul Hawken and Janine Benyus.

Dina: I cried. I admit it [laughs]. It was really moving. Literally, I cried because we all lost somebody too young. I mean, we needed him longer, not that he was that young [seventy-seven], but that we needed more like him. We still do.

CHAPTER 10

"First, go to the coast, visit a river, explore the world, and learn about why biodiversity is important."

Photo by Maryann Mahood

Dr. Mark Westneat

Oceanic Voyager

Marine Biologist

University of Chicago

My first recollection of meeting Mark Westneat was wandering around the Holden Annex dormitory as a new student on the campus of the College of Wooster in Wooster, Ohio. We were hallmates our first year and fraternity brothers for the remainder of our time there. Wooster is a tiny college, and the town, when we ventured into it, seemed even smaller. How I got there confounds me to this day. Only my dad, the former college professor, can properly explain it. Irrespective of that, Mark and I struck up a friendship that has endured all these years. Mark is unique in many ways but what drew me most to him back then was his intellect and sense of humor. We would have the most absurd and offbeat conversations and share even more bizarre incidents during that four-year span. Mark was a naturalist, in his own right, even back in the Wooster days. He would go on these excursions and tell us all about them afterward, which was as fascinating to us as it was puzzling. I'm not going to deny that we had external influences consistent with college existence and with pledging a college fraternity. Mark majored in biology, while I was a Spanish and international relations major. How we handled those serious subjects as distracted as we were by the partying demands of Phi Sigma Alpha is noble in its lack of nobility. For the record, he graduated cum laude with Honors and I graduated. In any event, Mark and his roommate, John Morlidge, had a unique college pet: Shrew. It wasn't really a shrew, which, for the record, is in the Soricidae family, it was just named Shrew. No, it was actually a massive gerbil, in the Muridae family. The pet gerbil brings me back to some of those bizarre incidents at Wooster. Mark and John's pet was a no-nonsense, unaffectionate, little rodent. He—it was obvious he was a he—had an innate animosity toward other creatures, especially cats. Despite the strict no-pet dormitory policy, I owned a cat named Ruffian. Now, mind you, Ruffian or Ruff, as she was also known, was well named and fearless. She would randomly jump me in my sleep, chase the janitor's brooms (which got her expelled), and eat cafeteria cottage cheese, for example. There was one occasion where Ruff had an inadvertent encounter with Shrew. Not only was Ruff not intimidated, she was a bit overly curious showing why felines are one of nature's top predators. Just another bizarre incident in the annals of Phi Sigma Alpha or a warped version of the *Taming of the Shrew*, er, gerbil, courtesy of Mark Westneat. No gerbils or cats were actually harmed during this event or the retelling of this event.

Mark went on from his undergraduate degree at Wooster to earn his graduate degree and PhD from the Zoology Department at Duke, earning many educational accolades along the way. And although we would get together on occasion in either North Carolina or in his adopted hometown of Chicago, it was only after I began understanding the anthropogenic impact on the environment that I truly appreciated what Mark was researching and what he had accomplished. By 1992, Mark had joined the talented scientists at the Field Museum in Chicago as a Curator of Zoology and had begun lecturing at the University of Chicago. He has since published or copublished 100 or more articles in his field, and traveled to some of the most remote reefs and coastlines on the planet. He was elected Group Leader representing the Field Museum for the famous Encyclopedia of Life database project, which was at the behest of Dr. Edward O. Wilson—the world-renowned naturalist, entomologist, and creator of the project. Mark's group was joined by some of the brightest minds from Harvard University, the Marine Biological Laboratory, Missouri Botanical Garden, and the Smithsonian Institution. The Encyclopedia of Life project was to identify all living species before the inevitable loss of species occurred. Frankly, it's hard to preserve species that haven't been identified yet. In 2013, Mark became a full-time professor in the Department of Organismal Biology and Anatomy at the University of Chicago. In that period, I also witnessed Mark's wedding to Melina and saw his deserved rise to prominence in his field.

Interview—2013

I invited Mark to join a discussion on sustainability for the second NEWH Green Voice program at the annual Hospitality Design Expo in Las Vegas. Mark joined three other speakers who I'd invited for the roundtable discussion entitled "Sustainable Hospitality in the Crossroads of Climate Change." For every NEWH Green Voice roundtable discussion that I've created over the years, I've invited someone from the scientific community. In 2013, Mark was that scientist. It has been my belief for a long time that tourism and hotels in particular due to the scale of energy and resource usage must begin to reassess all aspects of their business models. From land development to design, from employment to supply chain, from renovation to resale, everything must be challenged based on environmental footprint. No sustainable economy can survive an industry blindly reaping profit from our insatiable desire to explore the planet without a proper ecological balance in place. And we may have already passed beyond the tipping point. Because of his research and the knowledge of his field, I knew that Mark could frame a pretty good argument for why we need to embrace sustainability and preserve biodiversity. It may not have been what many in the hospitality industry were expecting to hear, but it was one they wouldn't forget. Mark had firsthand knowledge of what can happen to coastal communities that have overdeveloped, overfished, and overrun their capacity to maintain an environmental balance. He's explored waters that have become toxic to native fish species; he has studied the effects of climate change on what were once vibrant and diverse coral reefs. If there was any question as to his immense knowledge of fishes and their habitat, it was quelled at the Mandalay Bay Aquarium in Las Vegas. He and I decided to visit the aquarium since it was close to our venue at the site. Mark had direct field contact with a number of species swimming in the tank and shared a few of these experiences with me. It wasn't long before we had a few followers sidling us as we went through the exhibit, ostensibly thinking they were on a tour. And, unofficially, they were.

I was convinced that a biologist with his acumen could educate an audience made up of hospitality representatives. It could be argued that the future of tourism, the largest industry in the world, has a direct correlation to the future of our environmental landscape. Seated in a semicircle on a stage inside an air-conditioned, desert casino in a city battling for water to maintain its existence requires no further explanation. Preserving natural resources is not your average high-wire act for Las Vegas. Mark shared a very poignant story from his many travels about a community that had come to the conclusion that developers, fishermen, and conservationists were all on the same page. His point was that no tourists will come to a coastal area devoid of fish, with polluted and acidified waters, simple as that. He had an impact on the attendees of our Green Voice discussion—just as I imagined he would.

David: Did you ever think we'd be discussing biodiversity, climate change, and sustainability, from our humble beginnings as freshmen on the campus of Wooster? I even know a little about the jaw patterns of wrasses and other labrid fishes because of you.

Mark: Ha, ha, yes, I remember those days as a college freshman with fondness, we were a crazy bunch of clueless fools back then. But you may remember that I used to go fishing all the time in the local rivers and streams around the Wooster campus in Ohio, and it was actually those experiences as a kid fishing, hiking, camping that led me to become a biologist and start to think about these kinds of questions.

David: From your current role as a professor at the University of Chicago in the Department of Organismal Biology and Anatomy, and from your former as a curator at the Field Museum, you have done a significant amount of research in the field. What is the most unexpected discovery you've come across in your long career?

Mark: The most unexpected discovery that I came across in my fieldwork over the years was early in my graduate school days, actually during my first trip to the Australian Great Barrier Reef. It was during this trip that I first saw the sling-jaw wrasse—an absolutely insane fish that I was able to get video of to show that it has the highest amount of jaw protrusion among all fishes. It basically throws its face at its prey just like the alien from the movie of the same name, forming a big long tube with its mouth that it uses to suck in its food. I have some cool videos of this up on YouTube.

David: You were one of the chairpersons for the Encyclopedia of Life project—an ambitious venture to identify and classify all species. Few people understand that we've really only identified a small percentage overall. How successful was the project, and how many species do you estimate are yet undiscovered? What is the risk of losing species at the current rate of extinction?

Mark: The Encyclopedia of Life project is a great effort to summarize information about all species using the web. I had a great time helping develop that project back in 2006 and helping guide it for about six years. The project continues and is building information every day about the diversity of species on Earth. Most of the information we have about species is focused on a fairly small number, about half a million, well-known species. We have names for about two to three million species but for many of those there isn't much information. How many species are there? We really have no idea, which is both frustrating but also exciting because there's lots left to discover. Estimates of total species count on Earth range from ten million to something like one hundred million species, depending on if you include all of the bacteria, viruses, microbes, things like that—we don't have a very good count yet.

David: When I asked you to speak at our Green Voice program in Las Vegas in 2013, I wanted you to provide an overview of what is happening to our oceans and lakes to a general audience. It's not typical at a hospitality design venue to have a scientific assay of what we're doing to our marine environment, but people have always migrated to our coasts, and many of the world's largest cities border these bodies of water. It is so critical to have healthy oceans and coastal communities. Are there examples of places you've visited where development and ecology have been properly balanced? What are the most startling changes you've witnessed to our oceans over the past twenty-five years?

Mark: I agree—I think it's really important for scientists to communicate with broader communities, businesses, politicians, and the general public more often, so I enjoyed that Las Vegas meeting. It was great to talk about ocean research and threats there, and this remains a really key problem. The threats to our oceans and coasts are many: the worst threats are sediment runoff from agriculture, which smothers coastal rocky reefs and coral reefs, changing ocean chemistry due to climate change, with the oceans becoming more acidic, and a host of other pollution factors like plastics, rising sea levels, overfishing, et cetera. It seems that we people, despite how much we love the ocean, cannot help ourselves but pollute and destroy our own coasts in really disappointing ways.

David: If you had one green deed you'd like to see heeded, adopted, and passed on, what would it be and why?

Mark: If I could do one green deed, it would be to save coral reefs. I know that's a huge thing and it comprises more than just one deed, but if I could do it I would, because I know that coral reefs are the canary in the coal mine of our planet, and if we damage our planet to the extent that coral reefs are no longer able to live, then we have gone too far. But let's break that one really big green deed down into some smaller ones, some deeds that are practical. For myself, I'm trying to do small green deeds by studying coral reefs to try to understand the biodiversity there and to understand mechanisms of coral bleaching and why corals are dying due to bleaching. If I can help people understand coral bleaching and death and teach people about that, maybe that will be one small piece of the effort needed toward saving coral reefs. And what about green deeds that just about anybody could do? First, go to the coast, visit a river, explore the world, and learn about why biodiversity is important. If you convince yourself that the oceans, rivers, and waters of our planet are important, then teach someone else about that—maybe your kids, your coworkers, even your mom, unless she's a scientist and knows more about it than you already. Maybe that's really the green deed that is the most important of all: first teach yourself about a natural wonder you love, learn about climate change and the critical importance of biodiversity in our lives, and then turn around and teach someone else.

David: Do you feel we can reach a global sustainable fish catch? I remember reading *Song for the Blue Ocean* by Carl Safina, for example. His investigative journey exposed much of the problem with determining what a sustainable catch limit is and then getting international commitment.[1] It hardly seems as if we're making any headway. What is your assessment of the state of the world's fisheries? And what is the outlook for the return of species like bluefin tuna, grouper, and cod?

Mark: It is highly unlikely that we will ever achieve sustainable fishing in the oceans. There are some species that are being fished sustainably now, but overall the total global fish catch is completely unsustainable. The bluefin tuna will probably be extinct within our lifetime—mostly due to overfishing but also due to ocean warming and acidification. The grouper fishery will never be the same because groupers just do not get as big as they used to because overfishing has reduced the size of which groupers will reproduce, and the maximum size to which they can grow. Apparently the cod fishery is starting to come back a little bit off of the Atlantic Coast, but will probably never be a viable, large-scale commercial fishery ever again.

David: Can you explain the good and the bad behind fish farms?

Mark: Fish farms can be a very effective way of providing tasty fish to people without impacting wild fish populations and overall diversity of our marine and freshwater ecosystems. Species like catfish, tilapia, and salmon can be farmed effectively and with minimal environmental impact. However, many fish farms, like salmon farms in the ocean, release a lot of nutrients and are contributing to coastal pollution, algal blooms like red tide, and other problems. So, for example, most farmed Atlantic salmon is on the do-not-buy list for sustainable seafood.

David: You and I have had discussions before about the perilous effect of climate change. I've heard Dr. Woodwell [chapter 2] state that no more fossil fuels can be extracted from the Earth if we are serious about reaching a leveling off of CO_2 emissions and serious about containing warming to a two-degree Celsius increase. What have you learned from your years of research about the potential consequences of unrestricted GHG [greenhouse gas] emissions?

Mark: As a marine biologist, the most obvious impact of greenhouse gases that I have seen is the impact on ocean chemistry, in the form of acidification. Acidification is the lowering of the pH of the ocean so that it becomes slightly more acidic than it used to be. The effect of this is that it makes it harder for ocean animals to make their shells and their skeleton. Corals are animals that make a hard skeleton out of calcium carbonate, a white stony substance that forms their skeleton. It is very similar to the shells of clams and mussels, which also have trouble building their shells because of ocean acidification. So, if greenhouse gases like carbon dioxide continue to be emitted by humans at high rates, the ocean will become more acidic, and pretty soon none of the animals including the ones we eat and the ones we depend on will be able to survive. This is also thought to be one of the reasons for coral bleaching and the decline of coral reefs; both acidification and warm temperatures increase the likelihood that the corals will die.

David: Although I'm not a diver, and can barely float, I've read a lot about changes in the world's reefs like you described and have seen firsthand. Give me a worst and best case from your experiences?

Mark: I have had the chance to dive and explore some of the world's most pristine coral reefs including the northern Great Barrier Reef in Australia, the reefs around Palau, and isolated reefs in the southern Philippines. These are spectacular areas that show high biodiversity, lots of big predators, like sharks, still abundant, and high coral cover, with many healthy coral colonies. I have also visited highly impacted reefs such as those in the Florida Keys, the Bahamas, Hawaii, and reefs in Southeast Asia that are close to big population centers. The differences between these reefs are incredibly striking, with the worst reefs looking like a dead stretch of concrete with a little bit of algae on top of it with a few fish trying to pick through to find some food. It's kind of similar to the difference between a live thriving rain forest and the barren mud hole that is left after they clear-cut it. I really think that if humans can't somehow succeed in saving some of the rain forests and the coral reefs of the world that we will have failed miserably in our civilization.

David: I've been in a number of countries that have a fairly small environmental footprint compared to the U.S. and been confronted by natives who feel that we in the U.S. are mostly responsible for the anthropogenic changes to the environment. The numbers support their argument. I don't think we truly understand the world's contempt for our overconsumption of natural resources. When it comes to combating climate change, we have the most to prove, I believe. How can we in the U.S. take the lead in mitigating climate change?

Mark: That's true. In the U.S., we are a developed nation with a long history of overconsumption, and now we can afford to take measures to correct our past mistakes, even though most of the time we don't do it. So, it is understandable that developing countries and smaller countries are resistant to limiting their economic growth or their overconsumption of resources, citing our bad example as a main reason why not. The U.S. could easily be a leader in reducing greenhouse gases if we fully embrace alternative energy sources like solar and wind, and yes, perhaps, even nuclear, and finally put an end to the "digging up nasty stuff out of the ground and burning it" approach to energy.

David: Do you still stay up and eat mac and cheese at 3:00 a.m.? Sorry, I can't even say that with a straight face [laughs].

Mark: Oh yeah, I still eat a lot of mac and cheese, mostly early in the evening with my three kids, not so much at 3:00 a.m. anymore [laughs].

David: Do you have any mentors or environmental heroes who have inspired you over the years? Anyone in particular who helped you identify your mission?

Mark: My advisors in graduate school were fantastic and remain good mentors who have inspired me to advance my studies and try to make a difference in our understanding of the natural world and play a role in education as well. Steve Wainwright, one of my PhD advisors at Duke University, made a significant impact on me. He sparked in me the realization that biology was truly what I wanted to do and that I could earn a living at it. Being in graduate school forced me to grow up. I took off from Wooster barely a month after graduation to begin my graduate work at Duke, and the evolution of my career began early on at Duke. My first course was marine ecology; isn't that poignant to our discussion? I found Dr. Wainwright to be one of the most interesting persons I had ever met. He made me realize that biology was so much more than what I had experienced in my undergraduate studies. That the conciliation of biology, physics, engineering was possible, and I wouldn't have discovered that without Steve's passion for the subject. He also made me see that there is an artistic and creative element to science, which I had not conceived. He sparked my interest in biomechanics, which I have researched for over thirty years, and lecture on today. Really, Dr. Wainwright helped me change the way I think about the world.

John Lundberg, another of my advisors at Duke, had a profound effect on me as well. It was from him I discovered my lifelong obsession with the Tree of Life—essentially that there is a structure behind the interaction of all organisms.[2] Dr. Lundberg had dedicated much of his life to solving the puzzle of the Tree of Life, and he lit the fire in me, which burns in many biologists. It has certainly become a lifelong obsession with me also. If we discover the overall pattern of species relationships, we would understand biodiversity so much better, we could solve medical problems, we could solve conservation problems, et cetera. It is the framework for understanding a lot more about the world. Dr. Lundberg took me exploring in Venezuela and Brazil and a memorable expedition floating down the Amazon River for two months. John had that deep passion for his work that good educators have, and, in my case, it still resonates with me. These days I am inspired by my own students who always seem to be finding new creative ways to ask questions about the natural world and to have an impact on conservation biology.

Another biology professor at Duke, Kathleen Smith, left an indelible mark on me as well. She taught me the nitty-gritty process of collecting data and analysis that has benefitted me as much as anything else. Graduate school can be an emotional roller coaster for scientists in the throes of research. Kathleen showed me how to stay level-headed and calm by direct example. She had a real calming effect on me, and others. Dr. Smith, who is still on the faculty at Duke, ultimately became the department head—I can't think of a better person for the job.

Lastly, on a more personal note, my parents were my first mentors, for sure. My mother, in particular, gave me the yearning for learning and reading, specifically. She was a librarian and reading teacher, who had the talent to be anything she wanted. I can't imagine spending a day without reading something of interest. I think I got that more from my mom than my dad. My quest for discovering the inner workings of our world may have originated from one of Mom's library books. Who knows. I do know that it started at an early age for me. And, as a father now, that's taken on new meaning.

CHAPTER 11

"We can build and remodel buildings to produce more energy than they consume and power our cars to boot."

THE SAN FRANCISCO INSTITUTE
OF ARCHITECTURE

confers upon

David C. Mahood

For Successful Completion of Required Academic Standing
August, 2014, the Degree of

MASTER OF BUSINESS ADMINISTRATION
IN SUSTAINABILITY

Fred A. Stitt, Director, SFIA

Fred A. Stitt

Organic Architecture and Design,

San Francisco Institute of Architecture

The idea for this book is owed to Fred A. Stitt, founder of San Francisco Institute of Architecture, and my pursuit of an MBA from his institution. An MBA in Sustainability is not a traditional degree, which Fred identified twenty years ago. While it encompasses much of what a conventional MBA would entail, it adds an overarching theme of sustainability. And if you think about it, shouldn't all MBAs of the future reflect this concept? As I've suggested, there aren't any economies of the future that can be sustained without a healthy planet. Fred started SFIA in 1990 to offer green building and design education that he felt was missing from existing architectural programs. Additionally, Fred has founded ecological design conferences and green publications; he has authored close to twenty books on architecture and ecological design, including one of the most successful textbooks on nature-based design called *Ecological Design Handbook*, which has been translated into most major languages including Chinese. He has educated thousands of budding architects and counseled thousands more. He is a scholar of Frank Lloyd Wright, having met him, and having been mentored by a Frank Lloyd Wright protégé, Bruce Goff, in the 1950s. Throughout his distinguished career, he recognized the need for creativity and unconventionality. Fred garnered national recognition at a congressional ceremony and briefing in 2009 for his concept of providing free green building education worldwide, which exemplifies his uncommon approach to education. Along those lines, SFIA's advanced architectural degrees are offered to LEED Accredited Professionals at a discounted price, which, admittedly, drew my attention in 2010. I knew I wanted to continue to advance my sustainability education but I really wasn't thinking about a Green MBA. After reviewing online everything I could discover about the program and the institution, which has all to do with Fred's vision and experience, I enrolled. I knew it would grind me down and absorb time that I never really set aside but it became another milepost along my journey. I mean, a big milepost, like the mileposts that say you have another 265 miles to your destination.

The Green MBA program at SFIA took me close to four years to complete, which meant that I didn't set aside nearly enough time to finish it in two years or less. I hadn't been an enrolled student since my frat party days with Mark Westneat, and I barely set aside enough time way back then despite the fact that it was my only real purpose for being at Wooster. But the Green MBA pursuit became something quite dissimilar because it made me reflect and identify key moments that shaped my environmental passion. It brought me back to E.O. Wilson's books, Jean Beasley's turtles, GreenSage, Woods Hole Research Center, the worm farm, Barbara Filippone's fabrics (chapter 12), and Susan's and my journey to Indonesia. Through the twenty or more books and the chapter reviews of each, I opened up the closet of my detached experiences and put them down on paper. It was cathartic to be able to make sense of all of it. At one point, Fred had to counsel me to keep my tell-backs to a single page or I'd never stay on any consistent pace. Rereading *Natural Capitalism*, written by Hunter Lovins, Amory Lovins, and Paul Hawken, all of whom I'd met at various green conferences, was so much more important this second time because of my real-life understanding of a nature-based economy.[1] Additionally, I got to pay tribute, in my small way, to Ray Anderson, who was, to many of us, the greatest CEO on the planet, and who understood better than any other Fortune 500 executive the importance of correcting our flawed economic system. Fred obviously enjoyed my reflections also. A typical response from my tell-backs: *truly exceptional work; heartfelt and beautifully written; "A" grade.*

Interview—2015

Before I earned my MBA in Sustainability in 2014, I had reached out to Fred a few times to gauge his or any of his colleagues' interest in joining me for the sustainability talks I'd developed for conferences, mostly NEWH Green Voice. Fred had a lifelong interest in ecological design and accepted my offer in 2014 to address the topic. I was thrilled to have him join me for the third NEWH Green Voice at HD Expo in May. To both of our dismay, he had unexpected surgery days before the event and had to cancel. He was truly missed—imagine the potential of a roundtable conversation that included Fred Stitt and Tom Herlihy on the same stage. I clearly had. Ultimately, I trudged on and finished my MBA from SFIA that summer. My original thesis idea for the degree was a book concept called "one green deed spawns another" that would include me reaching back out to the dozens of people who I'd written about in the program. It soon became quite clear that I had to change my thesis topic or that milepost would become destination 2,650 miles ahead. Undaunted, I decided to do both. Before I had completed my degree, I began writing this book. I owe that to Fred.

The combination of Fred's Alameda, California location and his intense SFIA schedule required that we correspond in lieu of a face-to-face interview. Funny thing, writing a set of questions for Fred was like another SFIA Green MBA assignment. And I loved it. I got to query the instructor, the founder, and the visionary, of San Francisco Institute of Architecture, the world's first and still largest professional school of sustainable design and green building.

David: Going through the process of earning my MBA in Sustainability from SFIA gave me the rare experience of reflecting on the past and retracing the many uneven steps I took along the way. The program's book reviews and tell-backs helped me understand why I took them and how I became environmentally active. That introspection truly was the impetus for writing this book. So, I want to thank you for helping me corral my loose collection of thoughts and experiences into a narrative. Explain what ecological design means in your context as an architect.

Fred: It means primarily centering one's attention on the health and well-being of the occupants of the building and the environment that hosts the building. For generations, architects have focused on designing an impressive façade, then clearing the building site as a pedestal to show off their work.

David: Why do you think we've gotten so removed from mimicking nature's example for buildings and design?

Fred: Two main problems: The first is architectural education remains in the classical mode—to design for looks, not for solving problems related to improving human well-being and enhancing the environment. The second is that architects who have sought a connection with nature have had to work outside the mainstream of the professional culture and hence have not been widely published or acknowledged by critics.

David: For twenty-five years, you have been educating students on organic building design since you founded San Francisco Institute of Architecture; do you think today's students get this kind of training in mainstream design and architectural programs? Have our universities done a better job since you began lecturing on the topic?

Fred: No. The university instructors certainly give lip service to ecology and the environment but students are not given theoretical or technical instruction on how to design and build sustainably. Frank Lloyd Wright, for example, pioneered most of what we know as green building, but his work is rarely presented as a positive or instructive example. Often, quite the opposite.

David: Much of your research and instruction, including many of your published books, preceded LEED, which has now become the de facto standard for green buildings. What do you think LEED's strengths and shortcomings are from your perspective, knowing that not many architects have your purview on the topic?

Fred: The folks who created LEED were filling a great need, mainly a way to reward green building and provide an objective means by which "greening" could be quantified and measured. It's rather overcomplicated now, and still doesn't provide true simplicity for rating homes and other smaller buildings. But even while overdone these days, it's still a great value, along with some other similar systems.

David: As I have asked all others in the book, if you had one green deed you'd like to see heeded, implemented, and passed on, what would it be and why?

Fred: Primarily, undo the academic accrediting system that inhibits true innovation and the liberation of young minds. Education hasn't changed in over 100 years and many of the most creative people of all time and our time are those who managed to create their own educations. This is particularly true in the world of green building and sustainable design.

David: The conflict between a traditional economic theory and a natural capital economy was a frequent topic within the MBA program material. I guess if you've never factored in the true cost of what the environment provides in terms of resources, you can't imagine anything flawed about our current economy despite the lessons of the industrial revolution. How do we shift to an economic model that puts a price tag on the role of natural resources in it?

Fred: I'm a Libertarian, and historic experience suggests that values are determined by the spread of knowledge and the many subsequent individual choices in the marketplace. People who learn about it, choose ecology and sustainability as a value, will make the best collective choices. In most instances, the choices should remain free of politics, otherwise very unwise policies become enacted as law. For example, many years ago the "energy crisis," which was created by politicians, led to many counterproductive energy-saving laws and massive numbers of subsidized, defective, rooftop solar water heaters. Similarly, today, many buildings are required to be insulated and sealed where there is no need for it and as a result are sealed so that interior air is guaranteed to accumulate and cause illness among occupants.

David: You have been a pioneer of organic architecture, and you have said that you were strongly influenced by Frank Lloyd Wright; how did he influence your vision of building design?

Fred: I'm finishing a book called *Frank Lloyd Wright Green* that will tell the story. From site and nature sensitivity to green roofs, daylighting, natural, nontoxic building materials, natural heating and cooling systems, and nature-based design proportioning, Mr. Wright did all that could possibly be done to green his architecture, and I admired it since I first saw it, when I was a boy of sixteen.[2] The architectural profession at large, on the other hand, found his work to be laughable.

David: Many of us have been taught simple lessons at an early age about ecology that we've never forgotten. My parents had solar panels put on our house in the seventies, which are still operating—fortunately the Reagan administration didn't come and take them down—and they planted trees and more trees, drove small cars, and implored us to waste not, in general. Lessons not lost on me today. Did you have early experiences that helped shape your long-standing commitment to sustainable living?

Fred: I was fortunate to be able to spend my childhood skipping school and roaming free in the foothills and dry washes of eastern Los Angeles. I enjoyed the natural environment, enjoyed my independence, and I appreciated the independent souls in Los Angeles—from the rocket guys at Cal Tech, to the sun lovers of Malibu and Venice, to the creative spirits of Hollywood.

David: As we continue to build and develop in regions limited in natural resources like fresh water, can architecture adapt to environmental crises and be a part of the solution?

Fred: Buildings are the primary sources of power consumption, pollution, long-term environmental toxicity, and wasted natural resources. It's not too much to say that they are the problem and potentially they are the solution. We can build and remodel buildings to produce more energy than they consume and power our cars to boot. They can clean the air, conserve water, and improve the productivity and well-being of their occupants. No special subsidies are required. Green buildings pay for and sell themselves.

David: What is the most innovative building or product design you've seen in your long, esteemed career?

Fred: I've long visited, appreciated, and taught about all the world's greatest historic architecture, but innovation in the way we understand it isn't among the values of that tradition. And to that point, the work of Frank Lloyd Wright, Antonio Gaudi, Art Nouveau, Bruce Goff, the Green Brothers, Bucky Fuller, and the many protégés of Mr. Wright may not be appreciated for their innovation. These days I find the same spirit animates the leading innovators of Silicon Valley. And their intellectual and product designs are fabulous and enhancing the education and lives of hundreds of millions of people worldwide. Steve Jobs [cofounder, Apple Inc., 1955–2011], an admirer of Mr. Wright, said quite correctly: "*Design* is a funny word. Some people think design means how it looks. But of course, if you dig deeper, it is really how it works." I've espoused that concept for decades now.[3]

CHAPTER 12

"But the point to all of this is that I came to realize that one person can make a really big difference."

Photo by Maryann Mahood

Barbara Filippone

Fiber Farmer

Hemp Advocate

EnviroTextiles

Sometimes it seems to me as if I've known Barbara Filippone most of my life. It's a mere sixteen years but we've packed a lot into that stretch of time. Olive Designs hadn't produced any furniture when I first reached out to Barbara in 1999. I was aware of hemp as a sustainable fabric source but I knew little of its characteristics and application. I got my hands on a gorgeous swatch of hemp fabric from a company called Hemp Textiles International. One phone call later, I was given Barbara's phone number. My first phone call with Barbara lasted an hour, and most have ever since. Perhaps that's why it seems I've known her so long. It isn't a matter of verbosity, she's just an interesting person. My first call with Barbara was unlike anything I'd ever experienced. She was passionate, she was knowledgeable, and she was definitely original. But there was a specific reason that I was directed to Barbara. She was the designer and developer of most of the luxury hemp and hemp blend fabrics being sold in the apparel and commercial markets. Her knowledge of hemp fabrics was far beyond anyone else's in the textile industry. We created a swatch card of a rich, natural, undyed 100% hemp textile. Our sample lounge chairs upholstered in this textile were stunning; notwithstanding the fact that the fabric was the most sustainable on the market. That didn't mean it sold for us, however. In 2000, the market for green commercial fabrics was in its infancy, and only a handful of companies grasped the importance of natural fibers.

Barbara founded EnviroTextiles not long after I started Olive Designs. She and her daughter, Summer, lived in Glenwood Springs, Colorado, at the time. They proceeded to establish the company in a former church, which is typical of Barbara's creativity. In those days many people sought out her knowledge of natural fibers. Her hemp fabric and yarn business was highly successful in the early 2000s but no hemp products could shed the counterculture marijuana connection, which has always stunted the commercialization of industrial hemp and prevented its legalization in the United States. As Barbara has often said to me, "Hemp is to marijuana as green pepper is to chili pepper." Anyone who has brought a hemp product to market will attest to the public ignorance of industrial hemp. For the record, hemp has less than 1% THC (tetrahydrocannabinol), the psychoactive ingredient found in cannabis. Its harvest can destroy a marijuana crop through cross pollination, so banning the growth of such a productive substance is counterintuitive, if not downright stupid.[1] All of the hemp fabrics we used for our exhibition samples at Olive Designs held up beautifully, confirming the legendary yarn strength of the fiber, as I witnessed when we revisited the chairs at Woods Hole Research Center. But this also had to do with Barbara's experience because many imported Chinese hemp fabrics did not consistently perform as well. Barbara Filippone became the face of hemp fabrics and the sought-after supplier to some top fashion labels, including Ralph Lauren.

Interview—2014

Polyurethane foam has been in the crosshairs of Barbara's creative vision for sustainable fibers. Her quest for alternative materials brought her to the agricultural communities of Mexico in 2006 where she came across a natural blend of coconut fiber and latex that could be modified for seating foam. Barbara, like me, believes that there are abundant natural alternatives to petrochemical products. And she can actually conceive and design a product from hemp, coconut, or another natural, native fiber. Many of these agricultural communities are remote areas inhabited by indigenous peoples. Few have gained sacrosanct status with these villagers like Barbara has done. To achieve something like that is far beyond making a charitable donation. It is to look someone in the eye, make a pact, commit, and follow through. Barbara successfully developed a CSR (Corporate Social Responsibility) program around one specific Mexican community. Her efforts continue to improve the community members' socioeconomic status—the work of one amazing woman.

Barbara met us in New York City in November 2014, at the same event, Boutique Design New York, where I interviewed Katie Fernholz for this book. Barbara chose at the last minute to come to support a seating company that manufactured a dining chair prototype using her natural fiber foam. We had secured a suite in advance at the Hotel New Yorker in case she wanted to stay with us during the show. I felt she deserved to be there, not only to promote the foam but to open people's minds to natural alternatives. Everyone who took the time to investigate the foam at the tradeshow was intrigued. There aren't many people in the hospitality industry who are fans of polyurethane foam, fire retardants, and flame barrier cloths. Petrochemicals require a more toxic solution to smolder and extinguish a fire, and the chemicals mount up. It is tantamount to the slow pharmaceutical poisoning of the body. Even if half of all the chairs in a hotel or restaurant were made from coco fiber and latex foam, it would have a profound effect on the overall health of the building and its guests.

The sixteen years of having Barbara as a friend, her "ascended male" friend as she dubs me, have been, at various times, joyous, tempestuous, and manic, but always familial and completely unique. This interview is the story of her remarkable journey and her undying faith in doing the right thing.

David: Your background is different than mine. Not many people have been as committed as you have been to natural fiber development, nor have the understanding of fiber like you have. How did you get started? How did you progress to the point where you're now one of the experts on natural fiber development?

Barbara: I'd say my mom, and being a kid. My dad said this last night to me [Barbara's folks reside in northern New Jersey, and she stayed with them before the tradeshow], "When you built your fort in the woods, you used to take the cedar bark from the cedar trees and you were using a wire brush and making curtains and braided rugs out of it. You had so much of it that I took it and sold it to the Boy Scouts as flint to supplement family income. I had mountains of it." And I remember it because I'd jump in it off of a rock. And then my mother—I must have been five or six years old—she took me to Little Falls in Paterson, New Jersey, which was a mill town.

David: You were raised in New Jersey?

Barbara: Yeah, my grandfather was a jacquard weaver who specialized in flax, so when I was a little kid I'd stay with my grandmother but nobody spoke English. My grandmother would take me down to the mills to bring my grandfather's lunch. I'd go in there and I hated the sound. I would cover my ears. I remember the machines like it was yesterday; they're all the same machines that are in Eastern Europe. My grandfather would punch cards—they were jacquard designs—and he'd make all kinds of beautiful flower designs. Later on in life, I was always drawing flowers, murals—I never knew where it came from, just being around it all my life. One day my mother picked me up from my grandmother's and she took me down to the river, and she said, "I want you to see what man-made polyester does." There were pipes coming out of the side from the road; I was seeing all this different-colored water going into Little Falls. I kept thinking this was making the water bad. It was my mother really who wouldn't let in polyester. I never even had a chocolate Easter bunny [laughs]. I was the only kid that had a pinyon pinecone that my dad would put in an Easter basket and say that when the bunny comes, you're going to have a surprise in the morning. He would bake the pinyon pinecones and there would be the pinyon nuts. So as a kid, it wasn't like a normal kid upbringing, you know [laughs]—it was a kid that had pinyon pinecones. My parents convinced us that ice cream was, well . . . I'd get a spoon full of Crisco, and told that's what ice cream was. My father was a real organo [avoiding use of unnatural chemicals]. My mother would say, "This is poison" . . . she would show me polyester, and say, "You can't breathe in this." She would take it apart and she would take the string, and I can remember her stretching this like a rubber band, and she would say to me, "It will make you smell and it's made with all kinds of dirty water you see going into the river." Instead of being told in a scientific way, it was more like *danger, you stay away from this*. But polyester is man-made, and when I learned the difference between a monofilament and a filament, all I could think of was fishing line. *They're taking fishing line and making clothing out of it, and we're supposed to put this on our bodies?*

I drew really well; I was a good drawer. I was nineteen—I guess I should say it—I dropped out of high school the last day of my junior year, the very last day. I got my GED, and I applied to Parson's School of Design in New York. I wanted to do repeat designs on fabric because I could draw. The very first one, which is ironic, David, was a turtle—taking off his shell and hanging it on a coat rack. I had this little skin of a turtle and I repeated the design and his little shell was hanging on that. I went to one semester at Parson's and then one at Art Students League. I think it's on fifty-seventh [New York City]...It was always art because that's the only thing I passed in high school besides English. Once, for example, my teacher caught me. Well, he thought I was cutting school and just hanging out being a bum. I took my thirty-five-cents lunch money and I would come into New York and see Marcel Marceau and Charlie Chaplin. While all the kids were doing their thing, I was the only weird kid sitting in the theatre. And it turned out my English teacher was sitting behind me. Once the show was over, someone tapped me on the shoulder and it was—I'll never forget his name, Mr. Iannacone—and he said to me, "I'll never fail you again." So, I got an A in Art and I got an A in English, and I failed everything else. Home economics, gym, math, science, history—I failed everything. That's why I dropped out of school, because I really wanted to do art.

David: But you've been able to take that, your artistic talent, and turn it into a very interesting timeline from that point. Once you left high school, what was next?

Barbara: I came into New York City. I was seventeen and I got accepted to Parson's…I got accepted…because my self-portrait was a drawing of my hand wearing a ring that I always wore. Everyone drew their faces and I just had my left hand. They said, "Oh, we accept her" [laughs]. I didn't like school; it was during the hippie era so I decided to go west. My father was very happy to get rid of me, I think. Anyhow, he got me a van with one of those fifty-dollar paint jobs where everything was the same color. I'm heading west, going to California, and I get to Grand Junction, Colorado…I'm filling up my gas tank at a gas station, and the gas tank falls off the van. It rusted right off [laughs]. Lo and behold, here come three cowboys; I had never seen a cowboy. I didn't know what they looked like, but they had ponytails with cowboy hats, and I said to myself, "Oh, I think I want one of those." One of them ended up being Summer's father.

But I had no real means of making money and my mother, well…she was a fabric addict who designed surface designs for Schumacher. She would also get into building houses and furnishing them, too. Anyhow, I was in Colorado and she said that she found some skirts on the street in New York. They were wrap skirts, *kurtas* they were called, and they were cotton. She and I agreed that she would send me a dozen—the skirts were two dollars and the shirts were a buck. I sold them all at the post office. I took them out of the box in

Palisade, Colorado, and sold all of them: six dollars for a skirt and four dollars for a top. I told Mom to send more. That summer…in 1975, I made $23,000. I was selling them in the college parking lots, at the state home, the mental hospital, anywhere. I had them in the back of my car. I went back to New York to visit my mother, and she brought me down on Broadway. It was called Hind India Cottage Emporium. She brought me to meet this man Monty. He sold sequin gowns and kurtas and wrap skirts. But there were only sequined gowns. The way I was dressed—I had made handkerchief shirts, and I had all kinds of weird hippie clothes and moccasins.

This Indian man said to me, "Can you make clothes like that?"

I said, "I don't know how to make them, but I can draw pictures of them."

Then he said to my mother, "Can we take her to India?"

My mother said, "Well, what are you going to do with her in India?"

He said, "Let her draw pictures, and we're going to make clothes."

Because it was cotton, my mother was approving of it. And I thought that cotton was something that was good and natural because we had two choices when we were kids: cotton and itchy wool. Not long after, I get taken to India. I'll never forget stepping off the airplane, and the smell was so bad that you couldn't breathe. I went to a place called Jaipur, the Pink City of India. I remember dead animals everywhere and the smell and the poverty—beyond anything I'd ever seen. But there was all this beautiful fabric, and they were drying it. It was all handwoven, and there were all these wooden poles. The fabric was drying in the sun almost like folded up and down over these rods, wood beams, and I asked someone, "What's going on here?"

One guy replied, "Well, we bleached it, and we're drying it."

I said, "Well, then what?"

He brought me to another place, and there were two men, one on each side of the table…The table was a block long, and they were silk-screening. One was pulling the ink across, and the other was pulling it across. And I thought *Wow, that's really cool, too.* I kept thinking every-thing was natural because of the cotton until I went to a place where they were dyeing it. It was cinder block or bricks, and there were these brick tanks, and they were dyeing fabric and there was a man standing in this vat, that was maybe a meter high, and he stepped out of the vat and from his knees down they were dyed black. It was a turning point for me.

I said to the man who was with me, the employer who employed 18,000 workers in India, "Why is such an old man doing this work?"

He said, "That man's younger than you."

And I was very young, but it dawned on me that that man had been standing in dye and he was riddled with disease and contamination. A lot of things happened like that. I was seeing workers in the hotels whose only good clothes were their uniforms. When you spend a month there you have no life, they work you to death, and I was seeing things that were violations of human rights. People so severe, so skinny, so hungry, and working so hard. For me, everything kind of came together. The night before, I got in trouble because I could hear screaming outside of my hotel and witnessed wild boars fighting with the people for food scraps being thrown out of the hotels. I looked down and there's this one woman, she must have had four or five kids, and she's carrying a handful of rice. I took the sheets off of my bed, and I ordered as much as I could off the menu and started lowering it off the balcony and I got caught. My boss told me that they're the untouchables.

David: Right, the caste system.

Barbara: There were a lot of lepers, but I didn't really know what lepers were, either. But that night I was taken to dinner and there was René Derhy, big designers like Horace Casuals, and all this India import. I was wearing a sequin gown with Birkenstocks because I didn't have the shoes. They asked me what I thought of their country.

I said, "Do you really want to know?"

They nodded yes. So, I said, "Have you ever heard of a barnyard? It's not just the cows that are sacred. I mean, every animal is coming in and out of people's homes, and that's filthy. The other thing is, do you know what a trash can is?"

They said, "That's for the untouchables."

And you were always up to your ankles in trash. Those were the two things that I recall the most. The next day I get called to my little workstation where you have six sewers, one pattern maker, and they said, "You have till ten o'clock in the morning." I thought to myself, *What do you mean? You mean ten o'clock at night* because you worked from ten in the morning till ten at night. Yes, they brought you your food but they worked you like you were a dog. Yes, you were in five-star hotels and treated like a princess, but the poverty and the suffering was unbearable. *Just unbearable to see this.* All the women ran the business offices and all the men were sewers. One day, the boss that I was working with went up to a man at his sewing machines and smacked him right on the back of the head and his head hit the sewing machine. I thought, *That's it, I'm not watching this anymore. I'm not goin' to tolerate it.* That night was when they asked what I thought about India that I referenced before. The next day, they got me there at quarter to ten, and I had one more fabric that I was supposed to complete—a collection of eight garments.

They said, "You have fifteen minutes to do this." I took scissors and cut it up, and that's how the godet skirt, the gored skirt came up. I cut it in triangles; I took straight pins and pinned it on the wall, and the next thing I know I'm being taken to an airplane. It's because I insulted them.

I get on the airplane and my name gets called. "Ms. Barbara, off the plane." I'm like, *Oh god, what did I do now?* I had a fork in my luggage. In Rajasthan you eat with your hands. I had forgotten I had brought a fork because I didn't like eating with my hands. Next thing I know, I'm stripped. They're looking at every orifice of my body because I had a fork. I'm like, *This country is upside down backwards and going in the wrong direction and they need to start over.* And I left. I left there and went to Las Vegas because I wanted to see my line called Her Style and American Angel. That's when I met David Stunda. I was walking down this aisle, and I see these three guys.

David: In Vegas?

Barbara: Yes. I had already seen my line, and it sold fifteen million dollars that show.

David: For what company?

Barbara: It was called Her Style and American Angel. There were three lines actually. Her Style was in boutiques and specialty chain stores, and American Angel was in department stores, and over a period of like forty-five days I did at least a hundred styles in six different prints. The whole time I'm thinking, *Oh, it's all natural, it's cotton.*

David: And you met the three Davids, not including me.

Barbara: Yes, that was before I met you. And I'm walking the show and I see these guys and I say to them, "Where are your samples? What happened?"

They said, "This is our sample."

I said, "What is it?"

They said, "It's a skirt."

I said, "For a pygmy?" I picked up the skirt and said, "Well, it would make a great hat." And I put it on my head and said, "What is this?" They told me that it was hemp.

I said, "What's hemp?" They said that it came from the Hmong Tribe in Thailand, and it was ceremonial cloth. They pulled out a whole bunch of rolls of it. Some was like butter, and some was really stiff.

I said, "What do they do with this?" They told me that they bury their dead in it. I thought that was interesting. I said, "Why don't you have any other clothing here?"

They said, "Well this is all we could make because it's only eighteen inches, twelve inches wide."

I said, "Well, I can make stuff out of it." Because I had just done the godet skirt. I said, "I'll design for you and you give me commission off of everything that sells."

They said, "It's a deal." So that was when I had the Hmong Tribe hemp, and it was all different ages and qualities...I designed a few things, and there was a guy in Thailand that took the drawings and had garments made. And then, one of the Davids said that there's some hemp that came from China made into only one fabric and it was called "summer cloth." It was really stiff; it looked like burlap or almost like burlap. He gave it to me, and I took it home and I asked my mom about how to bleach something without bleach. But I had used Clorox, too, so I took two buckets and I put this summer cloth in the Clorox bleach and I took hydrogen peroxide. The Clorox disintegrated the fiber. The hydrogen peroxide turned it like a creamy yellow and I thought, *Well, OK, now I can make something out of it.* In that period of time I was looking for a dyer and finisher. I wanted to import it, and in Denver, there really weren't any. So I found a company called Allegro Dyes. She, Sally was her name, was making wool rugs and she was using vegetal dyes. There were only five colors back then. I asked her, "Can we cut the fabric in piece length?" Because there was no dyeing machine, she was garment dyeing the yarn.

She said, "Sure."

And we put it in the garment-dyeing machine but there was no degumming, no removing the cellulose or lignin, and it clogged up the sewer system in Longmont, Colorado. Sally and I lay on the floor with our arms in the drain pulling this lignin and cellulose, and we're like, *Oh my God, what's going to happen here?*

David: Lignin is sort of a sticky resin.

Barbara: Oh, it was even thicker than a resin. It was almost like a balloon full of water. And at that period of time, she was trying to get Fieldcrest Cannon to convert to vegetal dyes. And it's funny now because this guy, John, who I'm currently working with, remembers that. That's when Fieldcrest Cannon went out of business—when they agreed to go 20% vegetal dyes.

David: Really?

Barbara: Yes, it was an eleven-million-dollar conversion for Fieldcrest Cannon. So that was like the early nineties.

David: That's a lot of money.

Barbara: Yeah, but it's kind of odd that they would go out of business shortly after that. So we did that line, and I had to use plumber's tape and mark each piece length with a waterproof marker to say this is a skirt and this is the top. Summer, my daughter, was only a little kid, and we were doing the cut and sew in a factory in Denver that was made up mostly of Vietnamese workers…Summer didn't even know that no one spoke English. I was also doing some subcontracting like the U.S. Ski Team's jacket and Marmot Mountaineering because I knew how to make commercial scale clothes.

David: By that point you had done a lot of work with natural fibers, and you were getting to a point where you could design a lot of different natural fiber products for not just apparel but for other applications as well. And it was a combination of your training growing up and your experiences in India and elsewhere that gave you this somewhat unusual expertise.

Barbara: See, I thought cotton was natural, but I didn't realize that there's terivoile that is also cotton. There was, it's hard to remember all of them now, but I discovered there's a lot of processing of harmful chemicals in cotton. I wasn't even aware of the growing of it yet.

David: And the water use and the pesticides.

Barbara: Well, see, I didn't know that yet. I still hadn't determined that. I kept reflecting on the man wading in the black dye and going, *Wait a minute, he's younger than me and he looks like he's ninety-two?* So we completed that line, and then the three Davids decided that they didn't want to do the business anymore—it was called Earth Goods—so I took it on, and I opened the very first hemp store with one fabric. And then I got headhunted but I didn't know what headhunting was . . . It was a woman from China who contacted me, and she said she was a student in America and she needed to find someone that knew about natural fibers. I said to her that I know about flax and I know about cotton and I know about summer cloth. And she wanted to take me to China. *Whoa, no,* I thought. She wanted me to open up distribution in San Francisco, and she wanted me to go to China to meet some people.

Well, they didn't speak English . . . The translator was in Canada and he would fly down, and then she—I don't know where she would go, she would come in and out . . . One day she said to me, "I'm taking you to China."

Now, I think that was around 1993, '94, and I believe it was right around the time of the world trade negotiations. There were no cell phones, no computers, and she took me to thirteen factories and five provinces in the land of Oz [laughs] because I didn't realize that no one had seen a foreigner. I didn't know this at the time. So then we go to this place called Hunan, which is in the south, and I really liked the factory. It was clean and there were schools and there was a karaoke hall . . . They walked me through the school of the workers and the kids, and the president of the factory was so proud because it was like "here he comes parading the monkey," which was me. Again, I didn't realize no one had seen a foreigner before. I have these photos—we're playing tug-of-war. There was only one fabric, so I get to this factory and they're making ramie fabric. I said to myself, *Well, I don't like that.*

David: Ramie is . . .

Barbara: Another plant fiber. It's very brittle and it wrinkles. It's kind of like tissue paper but stiff...They did some flax, and they said, "We have hemp" but they called it *da ma*. Da ma, cha ma, cha ma was flax. Da ma was hemp, and the same, sort of. And I told them that I know how to make these. I just sat down and started writing the math problems like my grandfather showed me. I saw it all my life. I didn't really know what the numbers meant but I knew what the cloth would look like. When I was writing those numbers, I really didn't know what was going to turn out but I still remembered them. For example, 18nm by 18nm by 45 by 42 57, and I just kept writing them...The Chinese kept making them, and they started calling them Ba Wa 1, Ba Wa 2, Ba Wa 3, Ba Wa 4, and it was Ba Wa.

David: B-A-W-A.

Barbara: Yeah, and we're getting up there [numbering system], so we decided to change it to *B*, which has been used now for twenty-three years. Yup, that's how long it's been used. So when I was at that factory, the real negotiations began at night after dinner. I sat in the lobby, and the woman who took me there pulled out a five-page Chinese character document— the only woman among all these men—and here she is insisting that I sign it. As I'm looking through it, in the characters I can see 1%, 2%, .5%, and I said to her that I'll have nothing to do with corruption. She got really angry, started screaming at me, but I told her that I'm not signing anything. And then we had this big fight, right in front of all these men in English, and nobody understood a word, and then she walks out on me, and all these men walk out, and here's the president of the factory sitting with me and he goes like this with his hands [throws up hands].

David: As in what's going on?

Barbara: Yeah, like what's going on. Neither one of us could communicate. Now mind you, no cell phones, no phone in the hotel, and no computers. I'm thinking, *I don't know where I am.* I really didn't, and I didn't know what I was going to do after she walked out. He brings me back to the hotel, and the next morning I go down to where the breakfast is thinking somebody's going to be there for me...Everything [food] in

Hunan is spicy. So I'm sitting in this dining hall going, *I don't know where I am or how I'm going to get out of here.*

David: Right, scary.

Barbara: Next thing you know, the soldiers come in, and I thought, *Oh my God*...The only thing I could think of doing is giving them the peace sign. Everyone knew what it was. The peace sign [hand sign]. So I go over to the table where all the food is, and I figure *Well, face fear,* you know? Anyhow, I am saying, "Is this spicy?" and waving my hand. And everyone's laughing at me because they've never seen a foreigner and here I am doing this.

David: Waving in front of your mouth.

Barbara: Yeah, then the driver came for me...I get brought back to the factory, and here is the president and Sunny, the woman who was with me...She comes walking in and sits at the head of the table, and that's like—well, you don't do that. If a foreigner is there, the foreigner always walks in the front. And she wouldn't translate for me. She refused to. So I drew a picture of an airplane and a stick figure and put Ba Wa on the piece of paper [laughs] because I didn't know how to communicate...I gave it to the president of the mill, and he goes off with the paper, and the driver gestures to me that we're going. He doesn't say anything, he's just leading me to the car, and he puts me in the front seat, which is really odd, and in the backseat is Sunny and this other man...We start driving, and she won't translate. I told her that "you have to speak to me and help me because I don't know where I am, I don't know what's going on." The best way to describe this is if you've ever seen the movie, *Karate Kid*, you know the part where that woman is doing the meditation with the snake—that's what it was like.

And we get to the base of a mountain, and this is really what led me to know that my heart was in China. There was a staircase going up into the mountains like as far as you could see, and she was walking ahead of me, which is not appropriate...The driver stayed with me, and we get to the top of this mountain...there's this temple and the entire temple is hand-embroidered silk. The walls, the floors, everything. There's no glass, it's just shutters, and there are two little hobbits. Really, they looked like hobbits, and you couldn't tell whether they were men or women. You couldn't really see well but I saw that the woman that I had the fight with is arguing with one of the hobbits and then she gives money to the hobbit…The hobbit [laughs]—I don't know what else to call them other than hobbit because they were so tiny—gives her big sticks of incense, and this woman Sunny goes into the temple…I see her bending up and down in the temple, and I'm kind of like *I want to do that* but I'm still standing with the driver. She comes out of the temple, and then this hobbit comes walking up to me and takes me in the temple. I couldn't see the face, it was just this hood. But whoever it was sits me down with my knees on these cushions and is holding my hands together with this incense and is making me bow like this [gestures]. And I'm thinking the whole time, *How am I going to get out of China? Where am I?* I had no idea where I was, but I was writing a diary too at the same time and I still have it. Fourteen pages I wrote. Anyhow, when I came out of the temple, that little hobbit looked up at me and if those weren't the eyes of God, I don't know what is. There were diamonds in that person's eyes. There were so many wrinkles that I couldn't tell whether it was a man or a woman. For all I know, now years later, that person had to be over a hundred years old, had to be. At that moment, I had this overwhelming feeling that everything's going to be OK. We walk back down the stairs, we head back to the factory, and the driver takes me into the big conference room where there's this very handsome Chinese man, and he comes up to me and tells me that he speaks English.

I said, "Oh good, I want to go to the airport anywhere."

David: Or "ahh, I need to get home."

Barbara: And he keeps saying, "I speak English. I speak English."

I said, "Well, how much English?" And I'm like, *That's the only thing he knows how to say. Great.* So again, I draw a picture of an airplane and a picture of me with the hair. I made the hair curly because the Chinese don't typically have curly hair…That man stayed with me for another day and a half before I was taken in a car to an airport. I get to this very small airport but there's really no airport. There's a man on a bicycle with a broom.

David: And this was nineteen…

Barbara: Ninety-three maybe, maybe it was ninety-two. It depends on who you talk to in China; I'll have to look at my passport. One of my passport books, anyhow. So here's a guy on a bicycle with two flashlights and a broom, and we're following him out in a field to get on an airplane...I'm standing in this field, and everybody's looking and laughing at me and pointing at me, and then someone spits on my feet. And I'm like, *This is getting weirder and weirder.*

Now I have no idea where I'm going. I get on the airplane, and the man that stayed with me turned out to be one of the principals . . . The president of the mill brought him to see me, to try and help me, thinking he spoke some English...I take off on the airplane with no idea where I'm going whatsoever. I arrive in Shenzhen, China, and there's two kids standing there with this sign that says "Ms. Ba Wa." I'm like, *Uh, am I still in China? Where am I?* I became ill. I started getting diarrhea, vomiting; I'm really, really sick...They took me to a hotel—at that time, I didn't understand the culture—and they actually stayed in the room with me and helped me. One of them spoke English and gave me a choice: Chinese medicine or American medicine. *Well, I'm in China I might as well have Chinese.* And they bring me snake fangs and something called watermelon mist. And, this may not have anything to do with textiles but it leads into what really your question is, because I'm meeting kindness, I'm meeting different forms of awareness. I didn't know that the watermelon mist, when you spray it in your mouth, makes your teeth black. It made me better but I had black teeth [laughs]. Then they told me that I needed to go on another airplane. I didn't know where I was going. I had no idea; I couldn't even pronounce the name. I arrive in Qingdao and here is Mr. D, and he looks just like ET, the extraterrestrial. He's got a growth like this [reaching out from head]. He's twenty-three years old. I said, "Who are you?"

He said, "I speak very good English."

I said, "Well, what are ya doin'?" I said, "What do you do?"

He said, "I work for Shandong Medical Supplies." I thought, *Hmm, I was supposed to be putting in a big order for fabric for Dong Ping in the U.S. and they were all my designs of the fabric.* Mr. D told me that he didn't know anything about Da Ma or Cha Ma. I asked him at that point if he wanted to learn about it. Anyhow, he asks me if I want to go to dinner and [said] that he would bring his girlfriend. She spoke English, too, and they also wanted to show the "monkey" around because there weren't many foreigners there before, either. And so, at dinner I asked Mr. D what he did for the company. He explained to me that [he] worked in import and export. I then asked him if he wanted to start his own company. He said that that's not possible. Well, after I told him that I had $300,000 that I'm supposed to spend on fabric, he gets up from the table, and he's gone for like fifteen minutes. He leaves the table and I don't know where he's going. It's like fifteen minutes. I then ask his girlfriend, who actually doesn't speak much English, where he was headed. She didn't know either. Shortly thereafter, he comes back and he's dripping wet. I asked him if it was raining.

He said, "No, I put my head underwater to stop the fire from coming out of my head. You changed my life. I make sixty dollars a month. You want to give me what? How many zeros is that?"

So I wrote down on a napkin *$300,000.00*. He actually had a red mark coming through the back of his neck. He kept saying it was fire. I thought, *Oh, come on, that's a pimple or something, but hey you never know.* So, he said that he would find a factory and start a business, and nobody had their own business back then. He located a factory in China, and we flew on an airplane that sucked my hair out of the plane. It was frightening because I knew it wasn't airtight because my hair kept trying to pull out the window of the airplane! And we get to this place—I didn't know where it was—a factory is a factory is a factory. It was twelve hours on the most dangerous road I've ever been on in my life. Just a dirt road on the side of a cliff and like only one car can pass, and it's twelve hours. This factory, it looks like everything's brown, and it's on one level. But then I go inside and it's state of the art and I'm like, *Huh?*

David: And they're making . . .

Barbara: Cloth. They're processing flax and hemp because they'd heard about the fabrics I had done with Dong Ping but they really didn't know what they were doing. There were all kinds of effluent water coming out and I was seeing slimy sludge that was built up, this green slime outside. But that factory became my home, literally, my home. So Mr. D takes me to this factory, and it's the first time in my career that I saw cleanliness, and I saw machines working, and people wearing masks.

David: State of the art.

Barbara: State of the art, where I've been told that everything is horrible work conditions and I'm flashing back on India. I'm in this incredible factory and thinking, *Well, OK, I want to work here. I don't ever want to go back to India.* And so I met President Lee and President Chen, and I ended up, well, I've been at that factory for twenty-three years. That's how long I've been there. And there have been only five foreigners there.

David: So, in a lot of ways that was the pioneering effort of all the hemp textiles that have been imported into the United States?

Barbara: All of them. Well, Dong Ping was the start of it. I think I had done thirty fabrics, just basics. What I did basically was copy cotton fabrics, the popular ones like jean fabrics. I wasn't doing T-shirts but jeans, trousers, women's blouses, and so all I did was use hemp to make the same weights and weaves I saw in India. I realized one thing though: it's up to the company. When people say that things are made poorly in China, that's a result of the designer and the instructions they provide.

David: That's right. It's the model they were given. You asked for cheap this, cheap that, and that's what you got.

Barbara: Yes, if they just say copy this, then the Chinese are going to copy it as cheaply as possible. So, all of my standards included guidelines for quality and consistency.

David: When were you finally at a point where you were comfortable with the product that was being made there, and that you were making inroads into apparel?

Barbara: Well, more, it was that I knew that I had to change what was happening to the waste, like the effluent water, for example. That was before they developed closed-loop [processing]. I didn't really know what it was called, but I said, "You can't keep dumping this stuff."

David: They've had a lot of issues with water and air pollution.

Barbara: And I remembered potato starch. And I suggested that we use potato starch as the sizing agent instead of PVA [polyvinyl alcohol] and PAA [polyacrylic acid]. Basically, just coat warps in potato starch. That helped the effluent water problem because the potato starch was like a fertilizer, and when it started coming out of the factories all the food that was being grown there started growing more. But I didn't know what it was called then. But the point to all of this is that I came to realize that one person can make a really big difference. If you give direction, and show someone the right way, then they're going to follow it. And, you know, you look at today and you think, *What are we doing, going backwards again?*

David: That can lead to the question that I've been asking everybody for this book. What is the one green deed you'd like to see people adopt, implement, and pass on, what would it be and why? And everybody has, of course, a different example of what that would be from their experience, but yours is so different.

Barbara: The one green deed, and I would say it to anyone, is that if you notice something that you can change, it is your duty to change it. It's that simple. Don't think you cannot change something that seems impossible because the person that you're going to change really wants that. And it's every organization's responsibility if you see a worker being hit or you see poisons going into the river to not turn away because if you have the courage to say just try this, people *will* do it. It leads to today, you look at what's going on and we hear that China is backwards? No, it's not. It may be a hundred years ahead of us. You look at India and not much has changed there. You still have the caste system. And then you look at my project in Mexico, and though I'm a small company, I make a difference. I see kids with no shoes who have no food when most of the executives go to a hotel where the room costs more than what it costs to feed seventy kids for a week—it's called corporate social responsibility. And if you don't do something about it, there's a hell where you're going. Because if I can do it, so can anybody else. And I've been feeding seventy-four kids for years—that's CSR [corporate social responsibility]. If you are sitting in a restaurant and you're seeing kids outside that are cold and hungry and you're in a developing country, don't throw that food out that's on your plate. Do something about it. And social responsibility is when you're building these big factories within a community, to support the community and its citizens. I'm teaching a community of Indians making pot scrubbers out of fiber, how to crochet, which has turned into the Beyond the Sun products. And we're now seven years into that project, and in seven years we've built a small clinic for wound care, and we've gotten a car for the teacher so she doesn't have to ride her bike six miles to get there.

David: By *Indian* you meant native, indigenous. Not to be confused with India.

Barbara: Right, indigenous. And it truly was an act of God because the person who was there before me was Anita Roddick [Founder of Body Shop] and she had died [2007, at age sixty-four].

David: I always admired her and the Body Shop.

Barbara: Yeah, well, L'Oreal purchased the Body Shop [2006] and then left the Indians with nothing after Anita died.

David: She would turn over in her grave.

Barbara: Right, six years those Indians didn't know why Anita didn't come. They didn't know what the Internet was. They never heard anything. Anyhow, I'm in this village with this guy, Gunnar, and it's late, I mean, it was nighttime so I couldn't really tell how primitive it was. The next morning I'm hiking down this path to go meet the matriarch—it's a matriarchal society. I walk into her hut and here's a picture of Anita Roddick. I look at the picture and point and say, "Anita?"

And the matriarch Mare falls down in her chair, starts crying, and she starts speaking and then says to Victor, my other companion, "I waited six years, and my sister and I had a dream a week ago that we were all going to starve and that we were climbing up a mountain and we couldn't get to the top of the mountain and we kept sliding down until a hand reached over the mountain, and it pulled us up the mountain, and that hand was you. And then we danced in the corn beyond the sun." And that's how Beyond the Sun products were born.

David: The label, and I've seen the picture, it's beautiful.

Barbara: Beautiful, and I'm not supposed to tell the story.

David: Well, we all have one green deed in us. Not all of us take the initiative but your one green deed was seventy-four lives let's say and then you multiply that out.

Barbara: By 150 and...

David: Imagine if everyone's green deed saved seventy-four people.

Barbara: It's doable. It is not that difficult and when I look at this community [in Mexico] and know that no matter what, they're mine for the rest of my life, it's doable.

David: And where is this in Mexico?

Barbara: It's in Hidalgo. Hidalgo is the smallest state in Mexico.

David: It's more central?

Barbara: It depends on how you draw it, but from Mexico City it's a day and a half north.

David: And a little bit east.

Barbara: Northeast, yeah. See that's my problem I never look at maps.

David: Well, I looked at a map. I know where that is.

Barbara: What's so unique about this whole experience is that it took us a while to start building up the number of products—about two years. There was a big ceremony one night, and I had two guys with me: one was my translator and the other was someone that I truly picked up along the way. I had 300 Indians come off the mountain and pray to me. And there is nothing more fulfilling in your life than to know that because you've taught people how to crochet, you've changed their lives. Even if it's a piece of bread, a band-aid, or whatever it may be, everyone has the ability to do this. And it's not always money.

David: Sometimes it's sharing. Sometimes it's kindness.

Barbara: Yeah! I always, whether I can speak the language or not, I always just walk up to people and talk to them like, "Hi, my name is Barb, who are you?" . . . They just look at me like *Huh?* But, it's a start. And it's like that in every country.

David: Well, we've been friends for a long time, and one of the things that's great about the ability to do this is that I get to share you and your story because it's important. People need to hear it--it's inspiring.

Barbara: Thanks, David, because everybody can do it.

CHAPTER 13

"It is really a profound shift from being isolated victims to a sense of our own power."

Frances Moore Lappé (L), Samantha Lovell (R) Photo by Jesse Steele, Small Planet Institute

Frances Moore Lappé

Purveyor of Hope

EcoMind

Small Planet Institute

n spring 2014, my stepdaughter Samantha called us from college to tell us we just had to meet this woman, Frances Moore Lappé. Admittedly, I had to look her up because I couldn't initially place the name. It didn't take long to recognize why Sam was so enthusiastic. Frances Moore Lappé is a tireless environmental and social activist who penned the best-selling book *Diet for a Small Planet*, in 1971, and has written or cowritten seventeen other books since. She has lectured at many esteemed colleges, appeared on major television networks, performed webinars and a TEDx Talks event, has received the prestigious Right Livelihood award (among many others), and has founded several organizations, including Small Planet Institute with her daughter Anna. And although I've not met her daughter, Anna, I've since learned that she is as formidable a talent as her mother. Frances Moore Lappé, or Frankie, as she is more commonly known, has received laudatory praise for her work by everyone from Jane Goodall, Barbara Kingsolver, and Vandana Shiva, to the late Howard Zinn. She even worked with folk singer Harry Chapin to combat world hunger in the 1970s up until his untimely death in 1981. She has been recognized worldwide for her contribution to food and nutrition and continues to serve on many prestigious boards. *Gourmet* magazine listed her as one of the twenty-five most important persons in history related to how America eats. And despite my fuzzy recall when Sam called us, Frances Moore Lappé is, in short, the most recognizable person I've ever had the pleasure of interviewing.

Frankie was doing a workshop for the environmental studies program at Colby College in Waterville, Maine, in 2014, which is how Sam became acquainted with her. At Sam's appeal, Maryann and I traveled up to Waterville from Beverly, Massachusetts, to hear a live performance from Frankie. She read from her latest book (at the time) called *EcoMind,* accompanied by a reggae band called Liquid Revolution. I was writing this book by then, and it dawned on me that I'll never cease to be moved by the environmental passion of others. Thus, this late connection was even more special because I was learning something new as a result of the next generation, in this case, my stepdaughter. And my journey now transitioned to our second generation: my sons and my stepdaughters.

Not only did we thoroughly enjoy the performance, we marveled at how easily she connected with the students and the younger audience in general. She was every bit as cool as she was dynamic. What a creative way of getting her critical message out into the public. If anyone in attendance left without having a far better sense of environmental preservation, they weren't really present. After the performance, Sam introduced us and mentioned my environmental interests and activities to her, which merited some added attention. She thoughtfully signed my copy of *EcoMind* and encouraged me to stay hopeful. I knew that I'd met someone very special, and I left that evening with the hope that I'd meet her again someday.

Interview—2015

I pitched my book to Frankie through her staff at Small Planet Institute in Cambridge, Massachusetts. Small Planet Institute was founded in 2001 to provide a voice and media presence for people on every continent who are creating living democracies through their empowered efforts.[1] After a series of emails, it was determined that after her latest book reached the publishers, she could fit me into her tight schedule. And I delayed the meeting further in the interest of having Samantha join me and reunite with Frankie. Through the diligence of Jesse Steele at Small Planet, we were able to make an August date work. The chance to pose questions to someone as knowledgeable and thoughtful as Frances Moore Lappé is a privilege. It affords you as a writer a lot of fertile ground to explore. Having read several of her books and a number of articles, I had a sense of her passion and her compelling argument about how we should grow food and how we should distribute it. The final stop on this journey was with the amazing Frances Moore Lappé, who has the unique ability to both inform and inspire and the courage to lead us to fight back as a fundamental principle of living democratically.

Once we all sat down at an upstairs conference room, I told Frankie that my mom, who holds a master's in Library Science from Syracuse University and has read more books in her lifetime than I'll likely ever get to, found *EcoMind* to be so uplifting and hopeful. Mom, like other wise and caring elders, gets beaten down by many of today's societal ills. She worries about the world that her grandsons will be inheriting. People in the latter stages of their lives need new forms of inspiration to combat the undulating feelings of despair. I shared with Frankie that my being there gave me the sense of doing something right by my mom. Frankie, a mother and grandmother herself, approved of that. I was also proud to be sporting a Small Planet T-shirt made from organic cotton, a small token of my appreciation. If there ever was a fountain of youth, Frankie spent some time in it. Or maybe there really is something to eating healthy, fresh, local food, as she has been encouraging us to do for forty-five years. She appears ageless.

David: I just read the twentieth anniversary edition of *Diet for a Small Planet*. With everything happening today, the message is still as critical as it was in 1971. Since that time, what do you think are the most important changes that have taken place since its original publication?

Frankie: Certainly I think that the level of awareness of the underlying causes of both hunger and environmental devastation is vastly greater. Nobody argues anymore that the cause of hunger is lack of food. Throughout the world are grassroots movements led by small farmers challenging the corporate-chemical-dependent model of farming. I just completed a new hunger book with Joseph Collins [*World Hunger: 10 Myths*], and while writing it, I became excited about how much more we know today about how to grow food ecologically.[2] Ecological farming practices are the only pathway by which poor people can end their own hunger and make a contribution to addressing climate change at the same time. But while we know so much more about solutions, the trend lines are pretty terrifying. In our new book, for example, we note that more people are getting the calories they need, although 800 million still lack sufficient calories. But calories and nutrition are parting ways. Many are getting enough calories but are still suffering. I tell the story in the first chapter of a doctor in India who said that he treats 2000 very poor rural Indians every month. They do not lack for calories I was told, but that 60% of them suffer from diabetes and heart conditions related to poor nutrition. In fact, two billion of us are deficient in at least one essential nutrient. And that's no small matter. Iron deficiency is linked to one in five maternal deaths.

Since I wrote *Diet for a Small Planet*, the concentration of political and economic power in the world has continued to increase globally. Today, eighty people control as much wealth as half the world's population. At the same time, yes, social movements throughout the world in virtually every country are working to counter the trend. Given that both are clear, it is time in which each of us can make a powerful choice, to acquiesce to the dominant, destructive pathway or to trust ourselves as co-creators of the new. My life has had two interwoven threads that are impossible to separate—hunger and democracy. In the early 1980s, my sound bite became: hunger is not caused by scarcity of food but by a scarcity of democracy. How much truer this feels today. In 1971, we couldn't have imagined the degree of environmental devastation from agriculture, for example. That we would disrupt nitrogen and phosphorous cycles even more than we have the carbon cycle, in a way, and very few people aware of it. We hear a news report of aquatic algal blooms, for example. It doesn't sound too bad, but that term is actually referring to highly toxic—not just toxic to marine life but to humans as well. The euphemism *bloom* in that context is really crazy [laughs]. [Algal blooms are caused by nutrient buildup and in extreme cases create dead zones.] Neither could we have imagined genetically modified organisms in 1971, introduced with little independent testing and even less forethought. We know so little. That is what frightens me: the health and environmental effects are still so unexplored because we don't put public funding into independent research. Most of the research has been funded by corporations with a financial state in GMOs.

I spoke in front of the World Food Prize gathering when the foundation gave the prize in part to a Monsanto scientist and others in the biotech industry. I was invited by a World Food Prize Laureate, a distinguished scientist himself, to be on the panel—right in the belly of the beast, so to speak. I had five minutes and I worked so hard on those five minutes [laughs]. The gist of my message was that it's not just the seed, it's the system—that genetically modified organisms they reinforce: one accelerating the concentration of control of our food system, giving farmers even fewer choices and decreasing biodiversity overall.

This extreme assault on biodiversity, we couldn't have imagined when I was writing *Diet for a Small Planet,* much less the antibiotics overuse as those things were just beginning to be known. So trends are, on the one hand, so much worse, but, on the other hand, we have so much more evidence of what *does work*. This twin realization has led me to a clear decision: I'm redirecting my energies for the rest of my life to focus on the vision and democracy strong enough to address the roots of our interlocking crises—I like to call it "Living Democracy." In it, a set of values—the wide dispersion of power, transparency in public affairs and mutual accountability, not finger-pointing—permeate every aspect of our cultures. There's no other way to address hunger, climate change, species decimation, or any of our challenges, as long as citizens' voices are muffled by the megaphones of great wealth. I kind of retreated from this underlying question in a way when I took up the rewrite of *World Hunger: Twelve Myths*. The book's use was dwindling because it was so out of date. I spent two years completely rewriting it. Now I'm back and to be true to its core message: the last of the now ten myths is that power is too concentrated, and it's too late for real change. It's similar in a way to how I respond to that in *EcoMind* with concrete examples from around the world that ultimately demonstrate that we've got to step up and get money out of its dominant role in our political systems. That's what I've been working on this morning: a draft of an open letter on building a Living Democracy movement—what it might look like and how to begin a conversation with people. The exciting thing is that there are now groups like Sierra Club, for example, especially groups that are associated with specific issues, utilizing their resources in a common effort they call the Democracy Initiative, which includes unions and civil rights organizations, in order to focus on democracy itself. So I find it terribly exciting. We can't give up our separate issues but we can never succeed with them unless we succeed together in building a democracy movement. So that's a very long answer.

David: That's alright because that leads me to other questions. One that we can discuss is about the SAFE ACT [H.R.1599—Safe and Accurate Food Labeling Act of 2015].[3] I feel that this is about as basic a right as there is for consumers, to know what's in their food. In all the work you've done, how did that policy hit you? Somehow arriving at that conclusion that we didn't need to actually label our food for GMOs?

Frankie: It is perhaps one of the most extreme symbols of the concentration of economic power that has its grip on our political system. Do you know GovTrack [www.govtrack.us]?

David: Yes, both Sam and I do.

Frankie: It's really handy. I recently read the summary of this act. I was really distressed that you had to study the abstract of the law to understand what it was really going to do. It was so misleading. We need to pass a law that would require some kind of accuracy in labeling of legislation. The bottom line is that the industry has been able to put forth this message that there is a consensus that GMOs are safe when there is no consensus. By the way, we have a fact sheet on GMOs that we're really proud of because it is backed by peer-reviewed evidence. It is not just an opinion piece.

David: I've seen it.

Frankie: One of the things I found most revealing of all the citations [on the Small Planet site] is the one that indicated that of the studies that have been done by industry on GMO safety that they found that there wasn't one funded by industry that uncovered any problem. Those that had independent funding—I think it was 22% or someplace between a fifth and a quarter of those studies—did find a problem.[4] That is not a scientific consensus, and most of these studies are not long term. They're very short term, and they've not been done in any way that we could see what is happening with human beings. Now we have all these increases in gastrointestinal diseases and allergies and other health issues, and we have no idea how to know whether there is a relationship. I totally agree that the right to know is a basic right, and that transparency is fundamental. I talk about Living Democracy being around really three, at least three, core principles: the first is the fluid and wide dispersion of power; the second is transparency in human relationships; the third is mutual accountability instead of the dominant form of blame game. As I say in *EcoMind*, if we're all connected, we're all implicated. So we can't just blame. A lot of my progressive friends really have problems with that. I was at dinner with some really dear people recently and I gave them my beyond-the-blame-game theory that if we're all connected, we're all implicated. Even the financial debacle of 2008—yeah, we can say it's Wall Street, and that would be true—but where were we as citizens when the rules got removed and Clinton [then President Bill Clinton] let that happen? We have to take a smidgen of responsibility that we weren't engaged as citizens to stand up and say, no, of course we need rules around the financial system to make it work. And this woman, who I really admire, said, "I'm not gonna take any responsibility." That principle that we're all accountable ultimately and we have to hold each other accountable. And yes, there are different degrees of blame and accountability but ultimately in a system's worldview then we're all on the hook. Nobody's off the hook.

David: I agree with that. I believe we're all implicated to a degree.

Frankie: The other thing I say is that nonaction is an action. It's a choice to not do anything, to remain ignorant. Of course, you know from *EcoMind*, and I know you believe this from what you were saying about your work and in the title of your book, that somebody's watching every single thing we do and somebody's always listening, and we're having an impact.

David: You were talking about antibiotics. It's in the food we eat and we forget that it's going to pass on to us. Sam knows this story. It's not really funny but I was stricken with *E. coli* [Escherichia coli] eating at an Arby's when I was twenty years old.

Frankie: Oh no, really, you have a personal experience.

David: Yeah, that was my only time eating at Arby's. I haven't really eaten beef or pork since. I used to tell people that it was because I never wanted to actually consume an animal whose head is as big as mine—thinking that it was funny. The reality is that these animals get tremendously stressed out in confined environments and are treated with antibiotics. Not just because they're stressed out but to make them grow faster. And we're eating it, not thinking that it has an effect on us. In some industries they've been able to diversify. Small and organic farms have been able to become successful and prominent in every community now, but it doesn't seem so much with the meat industry. We go to a local butcher, for example, because he has local products and offers antibiotic-free chicken. We think we're doing the right thing but do you ever think that there's going to be a movement to diversify the giant beef industry? Will we stop feeding them grain as you've been demanding for forty-five years?

Frankie: I don't know. I never feel like I can see the future. I'm not a futurist in that sense. Repeating what I said, I feel that a lot more people are aware that we are reducing our meat consumption, our beef consumption, certainly. In this new book, our second chapter is a climate change chapter saying that the myth construct is that climate change makes hunger inevitable. We're arguing in that chapter that there's so much inefficiency, so much waste built into our system, and that ecological agriculture is part of the way to address climate change. Clearly hunger is not inevitable as a result of climate change, and we pointed out the incredible inefficiency in waste and environmental impact of livestock. I'm hoping as that information gets out, whether it's health, environment, or just cruelty that people don't want to inflict, that most people will forever rethink their choices. We end up putting a brief section in the book on CAFOs [concentrated animal feeding operations] and the cruelty built into it. Even though it's a book about world hunger, we contend that it's all related. In a way, the blindness to the cruelty of the confined industrial agriculture model for livestock is a mirror of our blindness to the cruelty of hunger itself. This awakening has to come about together. I can remember when being a vegetarian for ethical reasons about cruelty to animals or environmental reasons labeled you as a freak. I mean, I was considered a kind of a freak. When people started reading *Diet for a Small Planet*, I would often hear people tell me that the main thing that helped them in the book was to convince their parents that they wouldn't die [by being a vegetarian] or become super unhealthy [laughs]. So we've gone from that point where it was assumed that we couldn't survive without meat to today where consistently now the medical authorities are telling us to supplant meat with more plant foods. There is a paradigm shift but it's just that the meat industry is still holding on. Actually, I was on Fox [Fox News] debating the President of Burger King Global Marketing.[5]

David: Too bad it wasn't Arby's [laughs].

Frankie: I was talking about this with my beloved partner and he said, "That was your finest moment." It was about an ad they put out. Anyway, what I basically said was that "yours [Burger King Ad Campaign] is really a bad business model." The guy really did look like a deer in the headlights. He expected me to do this big moral guilt trip thing but what I said is that it's a bad business model because people are waking up to this. I had kind of forgotten that I'd said that but it's on our website if you want to see me telling him that. But the bad business model is basically that people are waking up and this can't go on.

David: The exposure of these inhumane factory farms is on everybody's TV, in everybody's living room now.

Frankie: I still have a hard time personally understanding how people are such pet lovers and more and more devoted to their pets and yet can tolerate the absolute cruelty of the way we treat livestock and not have any cognitive dissonance there. That's a big piece that I don't get with the pet lover of America. It seems like we're pretty extreme in that way with our pets.

David: I love one of your quotes in particular from *Diet for a Small Planet*. It meant a lot to me and it's a lot of what I talk about in this book. You wrote, "Perhaps we can discover instead the real laws of the biotic community. In this discovery we can take joy in becoming contributing members not masters of that community."[6] To me, that's the crux of many of our environmental issues. Dr. Woodwell, who is profiled in the second chapter of the book, calls it the Golden Rule. I think it's this environmental ethic that eludes us and has eluded us. You've been espousing this for a long time. How do we move from the role of master to the one of steward?

Frankie: What I'm suggesting is that you can't be a member of the community if you're not familiar with it. My nine-year-old granddaughter and I did a workshop at a sustainable agriculture conference in Pennsylvania early spring. Our workshop was something like "We are guardians of the soil; we are defenders of the microbes." The concept was to learn about these members of our community by showing pictures of the different microbes and talking about what they did. When I was little, I didn't know there was anything alive in the soil. I thought soil was an inert substance. I think from childhood on, if we really start seeing life all around us, then the question is how do we keep all of that life alive? That's a very different question than just how do we get our sustenance. I hope we capture in our agroecology chapter in the new *World Hunger* book how important it is to learn how to work with nature. How it's challenging but it's so much more satisfying. It's ever-learning; not just following the rules from the chemical company that sent you the pesticides but actually examining the soil in your own farm. One of the things I did in the book is I quote the USDA [United States Department of Agriculture] on agroecology because as I was writing this book I was in North Dakota on Earth Day and the USDA had a big table at the student union where there were all these different Earth Day activities going on. There were these beautifully produced booklets from farmers about agroecology and organic agriculture—never mentioning those words. It was the most hopeful thing that I've encountered in recent years, because it said to me that it's permeating and that there were renegades inside the department. I talked to one of these renegades who I met at a conference much later. He said that farmers are just hungry for this information because the chemical approach is just not working for them. They're going broke. Most farmers are just not making money from farming. More and more, off-farm income is what's keeping farms alive. They're hungry for how to do farming another way.

David: They're restricted to monocropping practices.

Frankie: Right. So, I think that is the movement from being the dominator with our pesticides and chemical fertilizers to learning about your soil. Being an observer and a cooperator with the natural process is happening even within our U.S. Department of Agriculture. I hope our book [*World Hunger*] can help shift that mind-set because people still believe industrial agriculture is the dominant force but *we* are actually in control. One of the facts we put in our book, which I found surprising for Americans, is that we, U.S. industrial agriculture, actually feed fewer people per acre than Indian agriculture or Chinese agriculture. I thought that was pretty amazing because we think we're so productive. But we waste so much of it because we feed so much of it to animals.

David: I know for four decades you've been recognized as one of the most important worldwide voices on food, agriculture, and social change through your dozens of books, lectures, and appearances. You've inspired millions of citizens across the globe. It's an honor to have you in my book. If you had one green deed you'd like to see heeded, adopted, passed on, what would it be and why?

Frankie: Well, we're going to have to define *deed*. Most people think of *deed* differently, probably.

David: Action or concept?

Frankie: Well…to turn around, you know? To really turn around; it is a profound reframe. *It* meaning the solution is a profound shift of understanding of our own nature and our place in nature and what brings forth the best in us to align with the Earth. I think of it as the shift from our sense of self as disconnected from one another, and democracy or government as something done to us or for us at a distance, to really believing that we are capable of true self-governance and creating rules that bring out the best in us and keep the worst in check. And that we can create rules that keep power dispersed and keep the system transparent. If that had happened then the whole situation with Monsanto and GMOs would never have happened as it has. Further, that we create cultures from the earliest ages in which we all learn that we are co-responsible, where little kids are out doing their apprentice citizenship in their community and being a part of the solution so they understand from the earliest age that we are all contributors in either event: to the problem or to the solution. It is really a profound shift from being isolated victims to a sense of our own power, and that we evolved to be problem solvers and to be doers. I argue that our deepest needs beyond the physical are three things: connection, a real connection with each other. We'd die without that. They say the healthiest people are the ones who have the most friends and family, right? The second is meaning or a sense of purpose in our lives, which you obviously have in yours. And the last is agency, which is a sense of power and sense of voice. Thus, the reframe is to really claim our need for those, and to act from that context in everything we're doing and to have the guts to come together and say we have lost our democracy in this country or as I call it now, privately held government. Privately held government cannot address these crises that your book is addressing. We have to hear the true voice of every person. I stress *hear* because everyone may have a voice but if you're in an auditorium where most people can only speak in a normal voice while a few people have an electronic megaphone, then having a voice is meaningless. We have to have the right to be heard. That means that our voices and our votes have equal power. Not just with the few that literally have billions now to shape the whole terrain of the electoral ground. You have to have people who get it at that level, and are willing to speak out. Mike Brune [executive director of Sierra Club] is my new hero—he doesn't know it yet but he's my new hero [laughs]. He's somebody who can walk and—what is it we said about Gerald Ford back in the day—walk and chew gum? Anyway, we can have our issue and we can have our bedrock. We can have our single issue, maybe it's furniture, as you know well. And we can have that additional bedrock foundation that I am also a contributor to called Living Democracy. I call it Living Democracy because it's ever-evolving, it's not a structure that we just inherited. By the way, I've been reading a lot of history about our forefounders. They were unquestionably telling us that look, this is just the beginning, and every generation has to come up with its own. Jefferson [Thomas Jefferson] wanted every generation to write its own laws. They expected us and called on us to evolve this and use our common sense to improve on what they'd given us. So, this Living Democracy to me is ever-evolving. It's what you're doing right here by interviewing me and everything that you're doing by studying in school [gesturing to Samantha], both are a form of that. We are practicing democracy every day. It's not just something that we vote for to be *done* to us or *for* us. The green deed that is required of this generation that's alive today is that we are it, we are the deciders, and it is this frame shift that compels us to seek each other out and gain the strength to stay in that place and to keep coming back to it. No matter what our individual interest is, mine is food and hunger, and I'm not going to give that up, but my real emphasis now is going to be about Living Democracy.

David: I think there is a tremendous amount of sharing that goes along with sustainability. When we collaborate, and are connected, it demonstrates the act of sharing. I don't think you achieve sustainability without that act of sharing.

Frankie: Right. I guess my only caveat, the balance of it all, is this issue of people everywhere who are aware of the situation and who are trying to be a part of the solution feeling strained by these significant global and national issues. More, that the problems are beyond me, and it's all rigged, it's all broken. That all I can do is work my farm, and work in my community, but I really think that just isn't true, as much as we would like to just be able to say "I just can't deal with this." By our inaction, we've led to this degree of concentration of power, this incredible depth of suffering in poverty and environmental devastation—thinking that it's too big for me. It's further implicating us.

David: Not everybody takes the initiative to get their feet wet and go to places that have been ravaged by drought, poverty, whatever it might be, but you've done that. I had the opportunity to do a consultancy in Indonesia in parts of 2007 and 2008. It was eye-opening for me and probably was for you the first time you went to one of these places. We can't possibly solve global problems like deforestation of rain forest regions, which is where I was, without understanding the people who inhabit it. If you haven't actually been there and seen it, tried to understand the culture behind it, you can't possibly solve those issues. In your travels you must have seen this and gotten the opportunity to understand how other cultures live in regions that have been ravaged by drought, poverty, and ecological degradation. Did that change some of your outlook?

Frankie: Well by far the biggest effect was to just profoundly deepen my appreciation of what human beings—lacking all of the education and resources that we have—what they can accomplish. It gave me such deep confidence that in the right context people are so incredibly brave and creative. The story I've been telling now for a few years is about traveling to southern India a few years ago where I visited these women in part of the Deccan Development Society that I'd heard about in a number of places. These are the lowest-caste women, the untouchables, and they described their lives to me and it was dark, dark, dark. They were humiliated and beaten. They saw no future for themselves and were always on the edge of starvation. Within two decades the whole seventy-five communities totally transformed to biodiverse farming, absolute food security, and they had their own radio station sharing what they're learning. I asked about climate change, and they told me that they knew what seeds to use depending on rainfall, and that they weren't worried and were doing what they could. It's actually been meeting the poorest people on Earth who are showing us the way that has totally convinced me, and proved to me, that what I say is true because they're showing us that if we don't get in the way, people are incredibly resourceful. I think that now more women are coming forward, and the people who have most inspired me are female leaders. Particularly, I call her my lodestar of courage, now no longer with us, Wangari Maathai [1940–2011], who founded the Green Belt movement. I tell the story about how she started with seven trees on Earth Day. I told the story at Colby [College] about how ultimately teaming up with UNEP [United Nations Environment Programme] after she got the Nobel [2004 Nobel Peace Prize] that she got to thirteen million trees from seven. That's the biggest impact—convincing me that we can do this. We, in the industrial world, have a false sense of assuredness that we have the answers when the answers are really arising from people closest to the Earth who are supporting one another. These Deccan Development Society women, for example, meet once a week at 9:00 at night and make decisions in a circle so very much in support of each other. To me, that's how it must work. And I know that it really does work, and is working, so that's what keeps me going.

CHAPTER 14

A Confluence of Green Deeds

The Collective Vision

In fourth grade, as a quiet and introspective young boy, I wrote an A–Z alphabet book dedicated to ecology. Of course I didn't really know what ecology was at nine years old, but I seemed to be exceptionally moved by lack of care for our Earth. I've written numerous poems and articles with similar sentiment for decades, and this book is the culmination of that. The 1970s could be argued as the decade of the environment: from the first Earth Day to the Endangered Species Act to the establishment of the EPA, there was a groundswell of support for protecting Mother Earth during that period. My parents are both educators, so there was no lack of information and discussion regarding environmental protection at the dinner table. As it turned out, I wasn't as sullen and oblivious as I appeared to be, which for them has become a huge relief.

It seems as if we sway with the breeze like tumbleweed plants because we're not truly grounded as a species, and that awe we feel when we gaze at a natural landmark isn't connected to the caveat that we can lose everything by doing nothing. And there are many pertinent references: We allow our babies outside but we still choose to dump chemicals on our lawns; we don't see a drowned sea turtle when we eat seafood or a dead honeybee when we eat genetically-engineered corn. Or make the connection between monarchs and Monsanto or the one between Oreo cookies and orangutans. Cognizant of that, I think it's equally simple to take claims at their word as it is to condemn them without any credible assessment of real impact. Both are a disservice to the rest of us. In my fog of scientific ignorance, I've tried to rely on experts. I have tremendous respect for the handpicked environmentalists I selected within these pages with their diverse background and expertise. I'm not going to accept that our habitat is going to hell in a sun chariot without asking how and why. In our embrace of industrialization is the reality of habitat pollution and the bargaining of species. We reign as the one species that evolved into a role of dominance, able to use technology to eliminate other species and perhaps, unwittingly, our own. I've also learned that we're not all primed to destroy our fellow brothers and sisters but in fact are programmed to nurture each other. Yet, we're capable of so much more. One green deed is just a single finite action if we're not enjoined.

I've met some phenomenal people who wholly eclipse my efforts, and I gain such inspiration from their environmental commitment and dedication. I was so moved by the quote "The loss of biodiversity is the folly our descendants are least likely to forgive us," that I asked permission of Edward O. Wilson, the renowned biologist and author, to use it for my Olive Designs' brochure back in 2001.[1] His letter of approval hangs on a wall in our house. It was reading his book, *Diversity of Life,* especially the final chapters, that proved to be one of the catalysts of that epiphany I reference so much. He eloquently expressed the sentiment that by reducing the diversity of nature, we are downgrading the experience of future generations, and that we're but one among millions of interdependent species that inhabit this planet—all of which play an important role in achieving ecological balance.[2] For the record, I was unsuccessful in gaining his participation in the book despite startling him and pitching the book to him in Charlotte Douglas Airport. Sorry for that, Dr. Wilson.

In late 1997 when I embarked on this quixotic expedition to embrace sustainability and reinvent my career, I was quite naive. Chasing down real environmental windmills is the proverbial act of naïveté, many of us have found that out the hard way. It's been a weighty task to convince others that we're not taking care of our planet and its inhabitants. Environmental conservation is not a political matter nor does it harm an economy that properly assays the worth of its natural resources. In the United States, the ceaseless debate over economy versus environment is inherently flawed because no economy can be sustained without a healthy planet. There are not two paths that continue on endlessly. To hear nonscientists like me make the case for global climate change stuck in the oncoming traffic of fossil-fuel-derived energy companies is akin to the Monroe Doctrine for Spanish conquistadors. But it never mattered to me then that I might fail in this mission or that I might not advance my career. I just knew that I couldn't go back. How could I possibly sell another chair laden with chemicals or a table carved from an orphaned tree from an orphaned forest? Or upholster a chair in anything other than a fabric like Barbara's sacred hemp cloth? How could I eat another morsel of food without knowing whether it was sustainably raised or planted or without knowing what the hell it was made from for that matter? How could I eat another Arby's roast beef sandwich (er, OK, a Big Mac) knowing that it required a dozen pounds of grain overall to produce, grain that could have fed a large family in an impoverished community? I refuse to eat fish without referring to a variety of sustainable fish indices and paying attention to researchers like my college mate, Mark. I understand the critical importance of composting organic waste better by meeting millions of red worms at the worm farm. As we watch the current Dakota Access Pipeline standoff with Lakota protesters facing off against a nation that turned its back on their people more than a century earlier, I reflect on the wisdom of Peter Jemison and his efforts to sustain a culture. The Haudenosaunee have a permanent place in my conscience because we share a territorial homeland. We have a responsibility to preserve Native American cultures for future generations. What a shame it would be if no one ever knew the heroic feats of Peter's eighth-generation ancestor. Tremendous progress has been made to reduce the environmental footprint of commercial buildings, which is a tribute to the dedication of educators and designers like Professor Fred Stitt and Dina Belon. Far from being low-hanging fruit, the concept of a green, living building has been conceived and developed. Years ago, LEED prompted an industry to redesign its future and, to its credit, inspired the next generation of architects and designers. All species, not just sea turtles, deserve cleaner water and beaches and a complete overhaul of mass fishing methods. There simply aren't enough Jean Beasleys to go around. The work associated with gaining my Green MBA from Fred's institution gave me a whole new appreciation for my early green ventures and the amazing people I encountered. I still am naive to a degree, but it's a different type of naïveté. Somewhere along the way I've gained faith. An instinctive faith—like the faith that an amoeba has that it will reproduce—I can't fully explain the process I just know that it's going to happen. I had an environmental epiphany, and anyone would be similarly affected as I have been all these years in the wake of this firsthand knowledge. I have since hosted, participated, and keynoted many environmental discussions since 1997, and I have spoken about sustainability on two continents. I've been a part of several businesses that espouse sustainability as a fundamental principle. I'm done talking with a slice of guilt wrapped around the demands for environmental preservation. We must all gather together and figure it out. It's there. In my fifth decade, I have less time now than I did wide-eyed in the 1970s embarking on an adventure that has erupted into environmental consciousness. I only know now that this is my life's work. And it has become substantially more important since I've become a father and stepfather. I'll never have to shrug my shoulders in their presence. I've done something, and I feel grounded knowing that I've shared my sentiments and knowledge with as many people as possible. If you aren't on your journey yet, welcome. If you are, share it.

Notes

Foreword

1. World Health Organization, "Tobacco Fact Sheet," *WHO Media Centre*, updated 2017, accessed March 31, 2017, http://www.who .int/mediacentre/factsheets/fs339/en/.
2. Jonathan Amos, "Polluted Air Causes 5.5 Million Deaths a Year New Research Says," *BBC News/Science and Environment,* February 13, 2016, accessed March 17, 2017, http://www.bbc.com/newsscience -environment-35568249.

Chapter 1

1. Alexandra Seltzer, "Morning Brings Record-Breaking Low Temperature, Warmer Day Ahead for Palm Beach County, Treasure Coast," *Palm Beach Post,* March 28, 2013, accessed September 26, 2014, http://www .palmbeachpost.com/weather/morning-brings-record-breaking-low -temperature-warmer-day-ahead-for-palm-beach-county-treasure -coast/bpHl9ojj3MwwBFITS55yWN/.
2. Gillian Spear, "Colorado Fire Now Most Destructive in State History," *NBC News/US News,* June 15, 2013, accessed July 7, 2014, http: //usnews.nbcnews.com/_news/2013/06/15/18975566-colorado -fire-now-most-destructive-in-state-history?lite.
3. Pamela Flick, "California's Rim Fire: Opportunities Rise from the Ashes," *Defenders of Wildlife Blog,* March 5, 2014, accessed August 16, 2014, http://www.defendersblog.org/2014/03/californias-rim-fire -opportunities-rise-ashes/.
4. Jason Samenow, "Deadly El Reno, Okla. Tornado Was Widest Ever Measured on Earth, Had Nearly 300 mph Winds," *Washington Post,* June 4, 2013, accessed August 18, 2014, http://www.washingtonpost.com /blogs/capital-weather-gang/wp/2013/06/04/deadly-el-reno-okla -tornado-was-widest-ever-measured-on-earth-had-nearly-300-mph-winds.

5. Kristina Pydynowski, "Death Valley Heat Breaks All-Time US June Record," *Accuweather,* July 2, 2013, accessed September 21, 2014, http://www.accuweather.com/en/weather-news/death-valley-heat -to-approach/14773174.

6. ABC 7 NY, "Rough Winter Sets Record for Flight Cancellations," *ABC 7NY,* May 14, 2014, accessed June 9, 2014, http://abc7ny.com /travel/rough-winter-sets-record-for-flight-cancellations/58600/.

7. Boston.cbslocal, "National Weather Service Confirms EF2 Tornado Hit Revere," *CBS Boston,* July 8, 2014, accessed September 21, 2014, http://boston.cbslocal.com/2014/07/28/national-weather-service -investigating-possible-tornado-in-revere/.

8. Weather.gov, "Historic Long Island Flash Flooding—August 12–13, 2014," *National Weather Service,* August 13, 2014, accessed October 12, 2014, https://www.weather.gov/okx/HistoricFlooding_081314.

9. Michon Scott, "Record-Breaking Rain in Arizona," *NOAA Climate,* September 10, 2014, accessed October 21, 2014, https://www.climate. gov/news-features/event-tracker/record-breaking-rain-arizona.

10. Doyle Rice, "Epic Snowstorm on Track to Set a Record in Buffalo," *USA Today,* November 19, 2014, accessed December 3, 2014, http: //www.usatoday.com/story/weather/2014/11/19/wednesday -weather/19261905/.

Chapter 2

1. Natural Resources Defense Council, "Reference/Link/ Profiles— George M. Woodwell," *NRDC,* accessed March 16, 2014, http: //www.nrdc.org/reference/profiles/prowood.asp.

2. Thomas L. Freidman, "The Real War of Ideas," *New York Times*, June 10, 2014, accessed February 21, 2015, http://www.nytimes.com /2014/06/11/opinion/friedman-the-real-war-of-ideas.html.

3. Pilita Clark, "FTSE Joins Blackrock to Help Investors Avoid Fossil Fuels," *Financial Times,* April 28, 2014, accessed July 9, 2014, https: //www.ft.com/content/14787a44-cef6-11e3-ac8d-.

4. Andrea Thompson, "Major Greenhouse Gas Reductions Needed by 2050: IPCC," *Climate Central,* April 13, 2014, accessed November 9, 2014, http://www.climatecentral.org/news/major-green-house -gas-reductions-needed-to-curtail-climate-change-ipcc-17300.

Chapter 3

1. Judy Chicago, "The Dinner Party (1974–79)," *Judy Chicago,* accessed October 6, 2015, http://www.judychicago.com/gallery/the-dinner -party/dp-artwork/.

Chapter 4

1. New York State Department of Environmental Conservation, "480-a Forest Tax. Law," accessed February 19, 2015, http://www.dec.ny.gov /lands/5236.html.

2. Dovetail Partners, Inc., "About Dovetail Partners: A Trusted Source of Environmental Information," *Dovetailinc,* accessed January 28, 2015, http://www.dovetailinc.org/aboutus.

3. Richard Louv, *Last Child in the Woods: Saving Our Children from Nature-Deficit Disorder* (New York, NY: Workman Publishing Company, 2005), 99–105.

4. National Public Radio, "Tribal Nations Map: Our Own Names & Locations," *NPR,* accessed March 17, 2015, http://www.npr.org /assets/news/2014/06/Tribal_Nations_Map_NA.pdf.

5. Paul Gruchow, *Grass Roots: The Universe of Home* (Minneapolis, MN: Milkweed Editions, 1995).

6. Aldo Leopold, *The River of the Mother of God and other Essays by Aldo Leopold,* edited by J. Baird Callicot and Susan Flader (Madison, WI: University of Wisconsin Press. 1991), 337.

7. Walter B. Cannon, *Bodily Changes in Pain, Hunger, Fear, and Rage: An Account of Recent Researches into the Function of Emotional,* Reprint (New York, NY: Appleton, 1920).

Chapter 5

1. Justine Sullivan, "Jean Beasley—2013 Ocean Hero Award Winner!" *OCEANA,* July 30, 2013, accessed September 22, 2015, http://usa .oceana.org/blog/jean-beasley-2013-ocean-hero-award-winner.
2. Charles J. Moore, "Choking the Ocean with Plastic," *New York Times*, August 25, 2014, accessed October 24, 2015, https://www.nytimes.com /2014/08/26/opinion/choking-the-oceans-with-plastic.html?_r=0.
3. Carl Safina, *Voyage of the Turtle: In Pursuit of the Earth's Last Dinosaur* (New York, NY: Owl Books, 2007), 1.
4. Valeria Chavez, "The Turtle Lady: You're Never Too Old to Find Your Passion," *The Odyssey Online,* August 2, 2016, accessed November 13, 2016, https://www.theodysseyonline.com/the-turtle-lady.

Chapter 6

1. Sandra Steingraber, *Living Downstream: An Ecologist's Personal Investigation of Cancer and the Environment* (New York, NY: Vintage Books, 1997).
2. David R. Montgomery, *Dirt: The Erosion of Civilization* (Berkeley, CA: University of CA Press, 2008).
3. Yvon Chouinard, *Let My People Go Surfing: The Education of a Reluctant Businessman* (New York, NY: Penguin Books, 2005).
4. Paul Simon, "Kodachrome," on *There Goes Rhymin' Simon* album (New York, NY: Columbia Records, 1973).

Chapter 7

1. *Toxic Hot Seat,* directed by James Redford and Kirby Walker, HBO, 2013, film.

Chapter 8

1. Dee Brown, *Bury My Heart at Wounded Knee: An Indian History of the American West* (New York, NY: Henry Holt, 1970).

2. Anthony F. C. Wallace, *The Death and Rebirth of the Seneca* (New York, NY: Vintage Books, 1972), 40–41.

3. James E. Seaver, *A Narrative of the Life of Mary Jemison, 1824* (New York, NY: Garland Publishing, 1977).

Chapter 9

1. *An Inconvenient Truth*, directed by Davis Guggenheim, produced by Lawrence Bender Productions and Participant Media, Paramount Vantage, 2006, film.

2. Dan Levin, "Study Links Polluted Air in China to 1.6 Million Deaths a Year," *New York Times,* August 13, 2015, accessed December 12, 2015, https://www.nytimes.com/2015/08/14/world/asia/study-links-polluted-air-in-china-to-1-6-million-deaths-a-year.html.

3. International Living Future Institute, "Living Building Challenge," *Living-Future,* accessed January 11, 2016, https://living-future.org/lbc/.

4. Drive Electric Orlando, "About-Drive Electric Orlando," *Pluginperks,* accessed December 14, 2015, http://pluginperks.com/about/.

5. *Who Killed the Electric Car?* directed by Jessie Deeter, produced by Chris Paine, 2006, DVD (Los Angeles, CA: SONY Pictures Classic).

6. Carl Sterner, "How California's Net Zero Energy Mandate Will Shift the US Construction Industry," *Sefaira,* December 23, 2013, accessed December 16, 2015, http://sefaira.com/resources/how-californias-net-zero-energy-mandate-will-shift-the-us-construction-industry/.

Chapter 10

1. Carl Safina, *Song for the Blue Ocean* (New York, NY: John McRae /Owl Books, 1997), 94–95.

2. Tree of Life Web Project, "About the Tree of Life Project," *Tolweb,* accessed July 16, 2016, http://tolweb.org/tree/home.pages/abouttol.html.

Chapter 11

1. Ray C. Anderson, *Mid-Course Correction: Toward a Sustainable Enterprise* (White River Junction, VT, Chelsea Green Publishing, 1999).
2. Fred A. Stitt, *Frank Lloyd Wright Green: How Frank Lloyd Wright Thought, Solved Problems and Pioneered the Art and Science of Green Building* (Alameda, CA: San Francisco Institute of Architecture, 2015).
3. Joe Eaton and Ron Sullivan, "Steve Jobs' Gardener Describes Mutual Appreciation," *SFGATE*, February 26, 2012, accessed November 7, 2016, http://www.sfgate.com/homeandgarden/thedirt/article/Steve -Jobs-gardener-describes-mutual-appreciation-3356392.php.

Chapter 12

4. David C. Mahood, "Hemp: Nature's Forgotten Fiber," *Interiors and Sources*, August 2004, accessed July 23, 2014, http://www. interiorsandsources.com/article-details/articleid/4081/title/nature -s-forgotten-fiber.

Chapter 13

1. Small Planet Institute, "About the Small Planet Institute," *Small Planet Institute,* accessed September 9, 2015, http://smallplanet.org/about/.
2. Frances Moore Lappé and Joseph Collins, *World Hunger: 10 Myths* (New York, NY: Grove Press, 2015).
3. Safe and Accurate Food Labeling Act, H.R. 1599, 114th Congress (2015–2016), accessed January 16, 2016, https://www.congress .gov/bill/114th-congress/house-bill/1599/.
4. Small Planet Institute, "7 Really Good Reasons to Rethink GMOs," Small Planet Institute Fact Sheets, updated June 9, 2016, accessed September 8, 2015, http://smallplanet.org/sites/smallplanet.org/files /Small_Planet_GMO_Factsheet_7.pdf.
5. FOX News, "Burger King's Flawed Strategy," Media Center (You Tube), December 9, 2008, accessed September 3, 2015, https ://www.youtube.com/watch?v=jD2FG-Zoigk.

6. Frances Moore Lappé, *Diet for a Small Planet,* 20th anniversary ed. (New York, NY: Ballantine Books, 1991), xlii.

Chapter 14

1. Edward O. Wilson, *Naturalist* (Washington, D.C. and Covelo, CA: Island Press/Shearwater Books, 1994), 355.
2. Edward O. Wilson, *Diversity of Life* (Cambridge, MA: Belknap Press of Harvard University Press, 1992), chapter 15.

Bibliography

ABC 7 NY. "Rough Winter Sets Record for Flight Cancellations." *ABC 7NY*. May 14, 2014. Accessed June 9, 2014. http://abc7ny.com/travel/rough-winter-sets-record-for-flight-cancellations/58600/.

Amos, Jonathan. "Polluted Air Causes 5.5 Million Deaths a Year New Research Ways." *BBC News / Science and Environment*. February 13, 2016. Accessed March 17, 2017. http://www.bbc.com/news/science-environment-35568249.

An Inconvenient Truth. Film. Directed by Davis Guggenheim, produced by Lawrence Bender Productions and Participant Media. Los Angeles, CA: 2006. Paramount Vantage.

Anderson, Ray C. *Mid-Course Correction: Toward a Sustainable Enterprise*. White River Junction, VT: Chelsea Green Publishing, 1999.

Anderson, Ray C., and Robin White. *Confessions of a Radical Industrialist: Profits, People, Purpose—Doing Business by Respecting Earth*. New York, NY: St. Martin's Press, 2009.

Benyus, Janine. *Biomimicry: Innovation Inspired by Nature*. New York, NY: Quill, division of William Morrow, 1998.

Berry, Wendell. *The Unsettling of America*. San Francisco, CA: Sierra Club Books, 1977.

Berry, Wendell. *Window Poems*. Emeryville, CA: Shoemaker & Hoard, 2007.

Bonda, Penny, and Katie Sosnowchik. *Sustainable Commercial Interiors*. Hoboken, NJ: John Wiley and Sons, 2007.

Boston.cbslocal. "National Weather Service Confirms EF2 Tornado Hit Revere." *CBS Boston*. July 8, 2014. Accessed September 21, 2014. http://boston.cbslocal.com/2014/07/28/national-weather-service-investigating-possible-tornado-in-revere/.

Brower, David, and Steve Chapple. *Let the Mountains Talk, Let the Rivers Run: A Call to Those Who Would Save the World*. New York, NY: Harper Collins Publishers, 1995.

Brown, Dee. *Bury My Heart at Wounded Knee: An Indian History of the American West*. New York, NY: Henry Holt, 1970.

Brown, Lester R. *Eco-Economy: Building an Economy for the Earth*. New York, NY: Earth Policy Institute / W.W. Norton, 2001.

Cannon, Walter B. *Bodily Changes in Pain, Hunger, Fear, and Rage: An Account of Recent Researches into the Function of Emotional,* Reprint. New York, NY: Appleton, 1920.

Carson, Rachel. *Silent Spring*. 50th Anniversary edition. New York, NY: Mariner Books, 2002.

Chavez, Valeria. "The Turtle Lady: You're Never Too Old to Find Your Passion." *The Odyssey Online*. August 2, 2016. Accessed November 13, 2016. https://www.theodysseyonline.com/the-turtle-lady.

Chouinard, Yvon. *Let My People Go Surfing: The Education of a Reluctant Businessman*. New York, NY: Penguin Books, 2005.

Clark, Pilita. "FTSE Joins Blackrock to Help Investors Avoid Fossil Fuels." *The Financial Times*. April 28, 2014. Accessed July 9, 2014. https://www.ft.com/content/14787a44-cef6-11e3-ac8d-.

Davidson, Osha Gray. *Broken Heartland: The Rise of America's Rural Ghetto*. Iowa City, IA: University of Iowa Press, 1996.

Davidson, Osha Gray. *Fire in the Turtle House: The Green Sea Turtle and the Fate of the Ocean*. New York, NY: Public Affairs, 2001.

Densmore, Christopher. *Red Jacket: Iroquois Diplomat and Orator*. Syracuse, NY: Syracuse University Press, 1999.

Diamond, Jared. *Collapse: How Societies Choose to Fail or Succeed*. New York, NY: Penguin Books, 2006.

Dovetail Partners, Inc. "About Dovetail Partners: A Trusted Source of Environmental Information." *Dovetailinc*. Accessed January 28, 2015. http://www.dovetailinc.org/aboutus.

Drive Electric Orlando. "About-Drive Electric Orlando." *Pluginperks*. Accessed December 14, 2015, http://pluginperks.com/about/.

Eaton, Joe, and Ron Sullivan. "Steve Jobs' Gardener Describes Mutual Appreciation." *SFGATE*. February 26, 2012. Accessed November 7, 2016. http://www.sfgate.com/homeandgarden/thedirt/article/Steve-Jobs-gardener-describes-mutual-appreciation-3356392.php.

Esty, Daniel C., and Andrew Winston. *Green to Gold: How Smart Companies Use Environmental Strategy to Innovate and Create Value, and Build Competitive Advantage*. Hoboken, NJ: John Wiley and Sons, 2009.

Flick, Pamela. "California's Rim Fire: Opportunities Rise from the Ashes." *Defenders of Wildlife Blog.* March 5, 2014. Accessed August 16, 2014. http://www.defendersblog.org/2014/03/californias-rim-fire-opportunities-rise-ashes/.

FOX News. "Burger King's Flawed Strategy." Media Center. *You Tube.* Accessed September 3, 2015. https://www.youtube.com/watch?v=jD2FG-Zoigk.

Freidman, Thomas L. "The Real War of Ideas." *New York Times.* June 10, 2014. Accessed February 21, 2015. http://www.nytimes.com/2014/06/11/opinion/friedman-the-real-war-of-ideas.html.

Goodall, Jane, and Phillip Berman. *Reason for Hope: A Spiritual Journey.* New York, NY: Warner Books, 1999.

Gore, Albert, Jr. *Earth in the Balance: Ecology and the Human Spirit.* New York, NY: Plume, 1993.

Gruchow, Paul. *Grass Roots: The Universe of Home.* Minneapolis, MN: Milkweed Editions, 1995.

Hansen, James. *Storms of My Grandchildren: The Truth About the Coming Catastrophe and Our Last Chance to Save Humanity.* New York, NY: Bloomsbury, 2009.

Hawken, Paul. *Blessed Unrest: How the Largest Social Movement in History Is Restoring Grace, Justice, and Beauty to the World.* New York, NY: Penguin Books, 2007.

Hawken, Paul. *The Ecology of Commerce: A Declaration of Sustainability.* New York, NY: HarperCollins Business, 1994.

Hawken, Paul, Amory Lovins, and L. Hunter Lovins. *Natural Capitalism: Creating the Next Industrial Revolution.* Boston, MA: Back Bay Books, 2000.

Hill, Julia Butterfly. *The Legacy of Luna: The Story of a Tree, a Woman, and the Struggle to Save the Redwoods.* New York, NY: HarperCollins Publishers, 2001.

Houghton, Richard A., and Allison B. White, eds. *Ecology and the Common Good: Great Issues of Environment.* Falmouth, MA: Woods Hole Research Center, 2014.

International Living Future Institute. "Living Building Challenge." *Living-Future.* Accessed January, 11, 2016. https://living-future.org/lbc/.

Josephy, Alvin M., Jr. *500 Nations: An Illustrated History of North American Indians.* New York, NY: Alfred A. Knopf, 1994.

Judy Chicago. "The Dinner Party (1974-79)." *Judy Chicago.* Accessed October 6, 2015. http://www.judychicago.com/gallery/the-dinner-party/dp -artwork/.

Klein, Naomi. *This Changes Everything: Capitalism vs. the Climate.* New York, NY: Simon and Schuster Paperbacks, 2014.

Kolbert, Elizabeth. *Field Notes from a Catastrophe: Man, Nature, and Climate Change.* New York, NY: Bloomsbury, 2009.

Lappé, Frances Moore. *Diet for a Small Planet.* New York, NY: Ballantine Books, 1971.

Lappé, Frances Moore. *Diet for a Small Planet.* 20th anniversary ed. New York, NY: Ballantine Books, 1991.

Lappé, Frances Moore. *EcoMind: Changing the Way We Think, to Create The World We Want.* New York, NY: Nation Books, 2013.

Lappé, Frances Moore. *Getting a Grip 2: Clarity, Creativity, and Courage for the World We Really Want.* Cambridge, MA: Small Planet Media, 2010.

Lappé, Frances Moore, and Joseph Collins. *World Hunger: 10 Myths.* New York, NY: Grove Press, 2015.

Lappé, Frances Moore, and Joseph Collins. *World Hunger: 12 Myths.* New York, NY: Grove Press, 1986.

Leopold, Aldo. *Sand County Almanac and Sketches Here and There.* New York, NY: Oxford University Press, 1949.

Leopold, Aldo. *The River of the Mother of God and Other Essays by Aldo Leopold,* Edited by J. Baird Callicot and Susan Flader. Madison, WI: University of Wisconsin Press. 1991.

Levin, Dan. "Study Links Polluted Air in China to 1.6 Million Deaths a Year." *New York Times.* Accessed December 12, 2015. https://www.nytimes. com/2015/08/14/world/asia/study-links-polluted-air-in-china-to-1-6 -million-deaths-a-year.html.

Linden, Eugene. *The Octopus and the Orangutan: New Tales of Animal Intrigue, Intelligence, and Ingenuity.* New York, NY: Plume, 2003.

Louv, Richard. *Last Child in the Woods: Saving Our Children from Nature-Deficit Disorder.* New York, NY: Workman Publishing Company, 2005.

Lovelock, James. *Revenge of Gaia: Earth's Climate Crisis & The Fate of Humanity.* New York, NY: Basic Books, 2006.

Maathai, Wangari. *Replenishing the Earth: Spiritual Values for Healing Ourselves and the World.* New York, NY: Doubleday, 2010.

Mahood, David C. "Hemp: Nature's Forgotten Fiber." *Interiors and Sources*. Accessed July 23, 2014. http://www.interiorsandsources.com/article -details/articleid/4081/title/nature-s-forgotten-fiber.

Mahood, R. Wayne, a.k.a. Dad. *A Strenuous Day*. Geneseo, NY: Milne Library, State University of New York at Geneseo, 2015.

Masson, Jefferey Moussaieff, and Susan McCarthy. *When Elephants Weep: The Emotional Lives of Animals*. New York, NY: Delta, Division of Dell Publishing, 1995.

McCool, Daniel. *River Republic: The Fall and Rise of America's Rivers*. New York, NY: Columbia University Press, 2012.

McDonough, William, and Michael Braungart. *Cradle to Cradle: Remaking the Way We Make Things*. New York, NY: North Point Press, 2002.

McKibben, Bill. *American Earth: Environmental Writing Since Thoreau*. Edited by Bill McKibben. New York, NY: The Library of America, 2008.

Montgomery, David R. *Dirt: The Erosion of Civilization*. Berkeley, CA: University of CA Press, 2008.

Moore, Charles J. "Choking the Ocean with Plastic." *New York Times*. August 25, 2014. Accessed October 24, 2015. https://www.nytimes.com /2014/08/26/opinion/choking-the-oceans-with-plastic.html?_r=0.

Nabokov, Peter. *Native American Testimony: A Chronicle of Indian-White Relations from Prophecy to the Present, 1492–2000*. 3rd ed. New York, NY: Penguin Books, 1999.

National Public Radio. "Tribal Nations Map: Our Own Names & Locations." *NPR*. Accessed March 17, 2015. http://www.npr.org/assets /news/2014/06/Tribal_Nations_Map_NA.pdf.

Natural Resources Defense Council. "Reference/Link/Profiles—George M. Woodwell." *NRDC*. Accessed March 16, 2014. http://www.nrdc.org /reference/profiles/prowood.asp.

Newbold, Heather, ed. *Life Stories: World-Renowned Scientists Reflect on Their Lives and the Future of Life on Earth*. Berkeley & Los Angeles, CA: University of California Press, 2000.

New York State Department of Environmental Conservation. "480-a Forest Tax Law." *Dec.ny*. Accessed February 19, 2015. http://www.dec .ny.gov/lands/5236.html.

Oreskes, Naomi, and Erik M. Conway. *Merchants of Doubt: How a Handful of Scientists Obscured the Truth on Issues from Tobacco Smoke to Global Warming.* New York, NY: Bloomsbury, 2010.

Pydynowski, Kristina. "Death Valley Heat Breaks All-Time US June Record." *Accuweather.* July 2, 2013. Accessed September 21, 2014. http://www.accuweather.com/en/weather-news/death-valley-heat-to-approach/14773174.

Quinn, Daniel. *Ishmael.* New York, NY: Bantam Books, 1992.

Rice, Doyle. "Epic Snowstorm on Track to Set a Record in Buffalo." *USA Today.* November 19, 2014. Accessed December 3, 2014. http://www.usatoday.com/story/weather/2014/11/19/wednesday-weather/19261905/.

Safe and Accurate Food Labeling Act, H.R. 1599. 114th Congress (2015-2016). Accessed January 16, 2016. https://www.congress.gov/bill/114th-congress/house-bill/1599/.

Safina, Carl. *Song for the Blue Ocean.* New York, NY: Owl Books, 1999.

Safina, Carl. *Voyage of the Turtle: In Pursuit of the Earth's Last Dinosaur.* New York, NY: Owl Books, 2007.

Samenow, Jason. "Deadly El Reno, Okla. Tornado Was Widest River Measured on Earth, Had Nearly 300 mph Winds." *The Washington Post.* June 4, 2013. Accessed August 18, 2014. http://www.washingtonpost.com/blogs/capital-weather-gang/wp/2013/06/04/deadly-el-reno-okla-tornado-was-widest-ever-measured-on-earth-had-nearly-300-mph-winds.

Scott, Michon. "Record-Breaking Rain in Arizona." *NOAA Climate.* September 10, 2014. Accessed October 21, 2014. https://www.climate.gov/news-features/event-tracker/record-breaking-rain-arizona.

Seltzer, Alexandra. "Morning Brings Record-Breaking Low Temperature, Warmer Day Ahead for Palm Beach County, Treasure Coast." *Palm Beach Post.* March 28, 2013. Accessed September 26, 2014. http://www.palmbeachpost.com/weather/morning-brings-record-breaking-low-temperature-warmer-day-ahead-for-palm-beach-county-treasure-coastbpHl9ojj3MwwBFITS55yWN/.

Shore, William H., ed. *The Nature of Nature: New Essays from America's Finest Writers of Nature.* Orlando, FL: Harcourt Brace, 1994.

Simon, Paul. "Kodachrome." On *There Goes Rhymin' Simon.* Album. New York, NY: Columbia Records, 1973.

Small Planet Institute. "About the Small Planet Institute." *Small Planet Institute.* Accessed September 9, 2015. *http://smallplanet.org/about/.*

Small Planet Institute. "7 Really Good Reasons to Rethink GMOs." *Small Planet Institute Fact Sheets.* Updated June 9, 2016. Accessed September 8, 2015. http://smallplanet.org/sites/smallplanet.org/files /Small_Planet_GMO_Factsheet_7.pdf.

Spear, Gillian. "Colorado Fire Now Most Destructive in State History." *NBC News / US News.* June 15, 2013. Accessed July 7, 2014. http: //usnews.nbcnews.com/_news/2013/06/15/18975566-colorado -fire-now-most-destructive-in-state-history?lite.

Speth, James Gustave. *Red Sky at Morning: America and the Crisis of the Global Environment.* New Haven, CT: Yale University Press, 2004.

Steingraber, Sandra. *Living Downstream: An Ecologist's Personal Investigation of Cancer and the Environment.* New York, NY: Vintage Books, 1997.

Sterner, Carl. "How California's Net Zero Energy Mandate Will Shift the US Construction Industry." *Sefaira.* December 23, 2013. Accessed December 16, 2015. http://sefaira.com/resources/how-californias-net-zero -energy-mandate-will-shift-the-us-construction-industry/.

Stitt, Fred A., ed. *Ecological Design Handbook: Sustainable Strategies for Architecture, Landscape Architecture, Interior Design, and Planning.* New York, NY: McGraw Hill, 1999.

Stitt, Fred A. *Frank Lloyd Wright Green: How Frank Lloyd Wright Thought, Solved Problems and Pioneered the Art and Science of Green Building.* Alameda, CA: San Francisco Institute of Architecture, 2015

Sullivan, Justine. "Jean Beasley—2013 Ocean Hero Award Winner!" *OCEANA.* July 30, 2013. Accessed September 22, 2015. http://usa .oceana.org/blog/jean-beasley-2013-ocean-hero-award-winner.

Suzuki, David. *The Sacred Balance: Rediscovering Our Place in Nature.* Vancouver, British Columbia, Canada: Greystone Books, 2007.

Thompson, Andrea. "Major Greenhouse Gas Reductions Needed by 2050: IPCC." *Climate Central.* April 13, 2014. Accessed November 9, 2014. http://www.climatecentral.org/news/major-greenhouse-gas -reductions-needed-to-curtail-climate-change-ipcc-17300.

Toxic Hot Seat. Film. Directed by James Redford and Kirby Walker. 2013. United States: HBO.

Tree of Life Web Project. "About the Tree of Life Project." *Tolweb.* No Date. Accessed July 16, 2016. http://tolweb.org/tree/home.pages/abouttol.html.

Wallace, Anthony F. C. *The Death and Rebirth of the Seneca.* New York, NY: Vintage Books, 1972.

Weather.gov. "Historic Long Island Flash Flooding—August 12-13, 2014." *National Weather Service.* Accessed October 12, 2014. https://www.weather.gov/okx/HistoricFlooding_081314.

Weisman, Alan. *The World without Us.* New York, NY: Picador, 2008.

Who Killed the Electric Car? Film. Directed by Jessie Deeter, produced by Chris Paine. 2006. Los Angeles, CA: SONY Pictures Classic.

Wilson, Edward O. *Diversity of Life.* Cambridge, MA: Belknap Press of Harvard University Press, 1992.

Wilson, Edward O. *The Future of Life.* New York, NY: Alfred A. Knopf, 2002.

Wilson, Edward O. *Naturalist.* Washington, D.C.: Island Press, 1994.

Woods Hole Research Center. "WHRC's Tour De Force on Forest Carbon." *Woods Hole Research Center Monthly Newsletter.* December 16, 2015. Accessed December 19, 2015. http://whrc.org/monthly-newsletter-december-2015/.

Woodwell, George M. *The Nature of a House: Building a World That Works.* Washington, D.C.: Island Press, 2009.

Woodwell, George M. *A World to Live In: An Ecologist's Vision for a Plundered Planet.* Cambridge, MA: MIT Press, 2016.

World Health Organization. "Tobacco Fact Sheet." Updated 2017. *WHO Media Centre.* Accessed March 31, 2017. http://www.who.int/mediacentre/factsheets/fs339/en/.

CPSIA information can be obtained
at www.ICGtesting.com
Printed in the USA
LVOW03s1505031217
558470LV00010B/691/P